**Vocational rehabilitation services
for disabled persons**
Legislative provisions

Vocational
rehabilitation services
for disabled persons
Legislative provisions

Handbook based on survey data
on legislative measures, experience and
research in 68 selected countries

International Labour Office   Geneva

ISBN 92-2-103015-6

First published 1982

Printed by the International Labour Office, Geneva, Switzerland

INDEX

Introduction

The International Labour Conference at its 65th Session in 1979 unanimously adopted a resolution concerning disabled persons. The operative part of the resolution called upon the International Labour Office (ILO) to lay stress on activities related to rehabilitation of the disabled which would be a contribution to the 1981 International Year of Disabled Persons. One of these activities was the gathering of documentation on legislation, experience and research in the area of vocational rehabilitation of the physically and mentally handicapped in member countries.

The Director-General of the ILO, in June 1980, accordingly submitted a questionnaire to member governments requesting information on their national legislative provisions for the vocational rehabilitation of disabled persons, covering vocational counselling, assessment, training, and placement in open or sheltered employment. Particular mention was to be made of the specific measures aimed at creating employment opportunities for disabled persons, including "quota schemes", specially designated jobs or reserved employment, incentive schemes, etc. In the absence of statutory provisions, a brief description of functioning national vocational rehabilitation services was requested. In addition, information was sought on the current and planned research in the field of vocational rehabilitation of disabled persons.

In response to the questionnaire, a total of 68 replies was received by the ILO from all regions of the world. The high response rate gives evidence of strong interest in a study of this kind and in international exchange of experience in a field of human and social services that is receiving increased attention.

The present study is related to an earlier study[1] which sought to give a general picture of the ways in which countries are approaching rehabilitation, to distinguish patterns of approach, and identify future trends in rehabilitation practices.

This volume, in a sense, updates the prior report, notably that section dealing with vocational rehabilitation provisions and services. The country replies are analysed and evaluated; in some cases, the information was supplemented by information available in the documentation of the ILO Vocational Rehabilitation Branch.[2]

----

[1] United Nations, Department of Economic and Social Affairs: Comparative Study on Legislation, Organisation and Administration of Rehabilitation Services for the Disabled, prepared jointly by the United Nations, the International Labour Organisation and the World Health Organisation (New York, 1976).

[2] These additional references included, for example:

United Nations, Department of Economic and Social Affairs: Recent Trends in Legislation concerning Rehabilitation Services for Disabled Persons in Selected Countries (New York, 1978; Sales No.: E.78.IV.1).

Comparative Study on the Rehabilitation of Handicapped Persons in the Countries of the Community; legal, administrative and technical aspects, Vols. I, II and III, Commission of the European Communities, 1974/75, Brussels.

(Footnote continued on next page)

The information is presented for each country, wherever possible, under the following headings:

Legislative Provisions

Vocational Rehabilitation Services

Employment (including placement services, open and sheltered employment)

Special Measures

Research

Future Plans.

In some cases, the information furnished was insufficient to cover all subjects, even with reference to supplementary sources. Moreover, some responding governments focused their replies on one or two specific aspects with less emphasis on the others. The information thus does not provide extensive analysis of the full implementation and effectiveness of the law. Nevertheless, the summaries as a whole reflect the situation as it existed in 1980/81. It is hoped that the study will serve as a guide and work of reference to rehabilitation professionals and that it will be of assistance to those responsible for drafting legislation concerning rehabilitation services for the disabled or in organising such services. The handbook is also intended to be an ILO contribution to the International Year of Disabled Persons.

All readers and users of this handbook are sincerely invited to communicate changes, additions and corrections regarding pertinent rehabilitation provisions in member countries to the ILO (Vocational Rehabilitation Branch), CH 1211 Geneva 22, Switzerland, so that they may be considered in future updatings.

(Footnote continued from previous page)

Legislation on the Rehabilitation and Employment of the Disabled, 1975, Council of Europe, Strasbourg.

I. SUMMARIES OF THE GOVERNMENTS' REPLIES

ANGOLA

1.   There   are   no   legislative   provisions   for   rehabilitation
services.

2.   Vocational rehabilitation services

The Department of Social Rehabilitation in the Secretariat of State
for Social Affairs (SEAS) is responsible for assistance to the
physically handicapped. Assistance is given mainly in terms of
material aids such as food, clothing, footwear, financial allowances
and transportation (e.g. wheelchairs).

2.   Employment

Those who can follow regular vocational training are integrated into
regular employment. Severely disabled and whose who cannot be
placed in regular employment work in small production centres
established by the SEAS on such tasks as needlework and other
handicrafts. In addition to vocational training and sheltered
employment, they also receive literacy training.

ARGENTINA

1. Legislative provisions

Act No. 22431 (1981) provides for a national system of protection for the disabled. This law contains both general and specific provisions. Similar provisions must also be adopted by the provinces to ensure that the system is uniformly and effectively applied throughout the Republic.

According to the new national legislation, a disabled person is anyone who suffers from permanent or prolonged physical or mental functional impairment which, taking into account his age and social background, involves a substantial handicap for his integration into the life of family, society, and into education or employment.

2. Vocational rehabilitation services

In the new system, two ministries are responsible for vocational rehabilitation: the Ministry of Culture and Education and the Ministry of Social Welfare. The former provides vocational training, social and individual guidance. To achieve its goals it collaborates with voluntary organisations and supports them financially. The latter promotes sheltered therapeutic workshops in the hospitals under its control.

3. Employment

(a) Open employment

Private undertakings that contract with the Government must give priority to engaging disabled persons who are capable of doing the work either independently or with occasional help.

A quota scheme of 4 per cent of the total workforce has been adopted. It applies to the State, its decentralised and autonomous bodies, non-state public bodies and state enterprises.

Employers of disabled persons are given tax exemptions which may reach 70 per cent of the wage or salary payments made to disabled personnel (including disabled homeworkers).

(b) Sheltered employment

The Ministry of Labour is empowered to set up, register and supervise sheltered production workshops and must encourage all efforts aimed at their implementation. As examples of the existing system, village settlements for the mentally retarded have been set up in rural areas.

4. Special measures

Free transportation by state-controlled public companies is provided to disabled persons to enable them to reach rehabilitation or training centres.

AUSTRALIA

1. Legislation

   - the Handicapped Persons Assistance Act (1974) provides for special facilities and services to those disabled children and adults who require sheltered employment, activity therapy, and other ancillary rehabilitation and service programmes;

   - the Commonwealth Employment Services Act (1978) contains provisions for specialised placement services to disabled persons;

   - the Social Services Act (1979) makes provision for the Common-wealth Rehabilitation Service (CRS) which administers a comprehensive national social/vocational rehabilitation service for the physically and mentally disabled.

2. Rehabilitation services

The Commonwealth Rehabilitation Service (CRS), which operates under the Department of Social Security, comprises a staff of approximately 600 professionals (physicians, psychologists, vocational counsellors, social workers, occupational therapists, etc.) They are responsible for specialised medical, social, vocational and educational rehabilitation services.

The Department of Social Security works closely with the Department of Employment and Youth Affairs which provides specialist employment officers and guidance counsellors for placing disabled persons in employment.

The Department of Social Security administers programmes of income maintenance for disabled persons, such as sheltered employment allowances (as an alternative to a disability pension), training allowances, and special incentive benefits to employed disabled.

The CRS also employs vocational instructors who provide job-related training and adjustment programmes in rehabilitation centres.

Eligible organisations which provide approved programmes of sheltered employment receive subsidies from the Department of Social Security.

Another special training scheme under the Department of Employment and Youth Affairs is the National Employment and Training System (NEAT). Work preparation projects provide pre-employment and remedial training to persons with a physical or mental disability.

3. Employment

There are no quota schemes, specially designated or reserved employment for disabled persons.

CRS counsellors consult with employer and worker organisations with a view to voluntarily creating employment opportunities for CRS rehabilitees.

The CRS utilises special on-the-job training and follow-up services (so-called "work-therapy") during which the employer does not pay a wage or salary to the rehabilitee but a training allowance is paid by CRS.

The Commonwealth Employment Service (CES) has offices throughout Australia which are responsible for assessment, counselling guidance services to disabled jobseekers as well as rehabilitation centres, disabled organisations and similar associations.

State Governments can issue "Slow Worker Permits" to permit the payment of less than standard wages to those workers whose productivity is lower than normal due to disability. These permits are designed to further the employment opportunities of the disabled in the open labour market. The permits require the consent of the relevant worker organisation and must be reviewed periodically.

Australia has an interdepartmental steering group to promote employment opportunities for the disabled in the Australian public civil service through special appointment and selection schemes.

4. Research

The Department of Social Security's CRS has developed an active information and resources development programme; a number of surveys on workshops, training centres and on programmes for special target groups (e.g. quadriplegics) have been conducted.

Another research project concerned applied advanced technology and bio-engineering contributions to rehabilitation.

A new survey in 1981 will seek to determine attitudes of employers, unions and workmates to disabled fellow workers.

AUSTRIA

1. Legislative provisions

    -   the Care for the Disabled Act (Text No. 183/1947) provides for
        vocational rehabilitation services to the civilian disabled;

    -   the General Social Security Act (No. 189/1955) and its by-laws
        provide for vocational rehabilitation in the framework of
        accident insurance and pension benefits;

    -   the War Victims' Medical Care Act (Text No. 152/1957)
        provides, among other things, for vocational training
        programmes;

    -   the General Social Insurance Act (Text No. 189/1955) provides
        for vocational rehabilitation and related services for work-
        accident and injury victims;

    -   the Tuberculosis Act (1968) includes rehabilitation
        programmes;

    -   the Labour Market Promotion Act (Text No. 31/1969) deals with
        specific measures for persons whose handicap affects their
        competitive position on the labour market. Handicap may be
        physical, mental or psychic. The measures provided include
        job adaptation, tools, testing of work aptitudes, preferential
        treatment in finding employment;

    -   the Integration of Handicapped Persons Act (Text No. 22/1970)
        contains specific obligations for employers (pt. 3 and pt. 4)
        and provides for the protection of the disabled against
        dismissal. According to the law, Austrian citizens with at
        least 50 per cent disability resulting from impaired health or
        a combination of more than one disability are entitled to
        protective measures.

2. Vocational rehabilitation services

The implementation of the Integration of Handicapped Persons Act and
of the Labour Market Promotion Act is the responsibility of the
Federal Ministry for Social Administration, the provincial offices
for the disabled, and the authorities responsible for job placement
and employment.

Each provincial (Land) employment office has a standing
Rehabilitation Committee.

Disabled persons are provided with vocational guidance and special
job training. The training programmes are carried out either in
rehabilitation centres or within enterprises (on-the-job training).
The number of training places has been increased by the provision of
new supraregional vocational training centres for integrating the
disabled in productive life.

3. Employment

Selective placement services are provided for disabled persons. The aim is to integrate them wherever possible alongside able-bodied workers. Several special measures have been adopted:

- subsidies to employers as well as to those disabled who wish to set up their own business;

- a quota scheme obliging employers with 25 or more workers to employ at least one disabled person for every 25 employees. The disabled must be Austrian citizens and have at least a 50 per cent disability. Employers who do not satisfy the prescribed quota must pay a monthly fine into a special fund (used to subsidise specific measures in favour of the handicapped). Disabled workers are given special protection against dismissal. Employers who exceed the quota of disabled employees receive premiums from the State.

As for sheltered employment, this serves two main purposes:

- on the one hand, sheltered workshops provide employment to disabled persons who are physically or mentally unsuited for work in the open labour market;

- on the other hand, sheltered workshops are workplaces which provide opportunities for certain disabled to develop, improve and recover their working capacities with a view to later integration in the open labour market.

A new network of sheltered workshops is being rapidly developed.

Thanks to a close co-operation between judicial and labour authorities, training programmes for discharged prisoners have been successfully established with the labour market authorities offering special placement and counselling services to persons discharged from penal institutions.

4. Special measures

Emphasis has been placed on accident prevention and sound organisation of work. In 1975 and 1978, ergonomic performance and requirement profiles were developed for use by company task forces in job analyses.

5. Research

Between 1978 and 1980, numerous research studies were carried out for the labour market authorities by different universities and institutes. They included:

- vocational integration of the disabled by rehabilitation counsellors and placement officers;

- occupational opportunities for the disabled in sheltered workshops;

- computer-assisted teaching;

- training programmes for various short courses for skilled workers.

Other research studies currently being carried out cover:

- the value of vocational integration for rehabilitated psychiatric patients;

- comparative studies of vocational training opportunities for blind and severely handicapped persons in Austria and other countries.

BANGLADESH

1.   Vocational rehabilitation services/employment

Although there are no legislative provisions for the rehabilitation
of the disabled, the Government has given increased emphasis to the
social welfare sector in the second five-year plan (1981-85) which
includes services to the disabled.

Some special measures include:

  - a Training and Rehabilitation Centre established in an
     industrial area near Dacca offering training, sheltered
     employment and placement services for the adult blind;

  - four Training and Rehabilitation Centres for the Physically
     Handicapped (known as "composite centres") created for deaf
     and mute as well as for blind persons. While education is
     provided to both groups separately, vocational sections in
     each school are integrated into a single unit;

  - a Rehabilitation Centre for the Physically Handicapped,
     consisting of:

       - a comprehensive rehabilitation complex with four
          components: an assessment centre, an apprentice training
          unit, which provides training in simple engineering,
          welding, spray painting; a placement service centre and
          an industrial production unit;

       - four rural rehabilitation centres providing training in
          rural crafts.

     Mobility training for teachers of the blind is also organised
     by the Centre.

Finally, the Government has sponsored a scheme for the establishment
of a centre for the treatment and rehabilitation of physically
handicapped children under the auspices of a registered voluntary
agency. The centre will also produce braces and prosthetic
appliances.

Disabled children are integrated into the programmes of regular
schools.

2.   Future plans

The Government is considering legislation to provide for employment
of disabled persons in government departments under a quota scheme.

BARBADOS

1. Rehabilitation services

There are no legislative provisions for rehabilitation of the disabled. Special education services for physically handicapped and mentally retarded children have been in existence for some time. Vocational rehabilitation services date back to 1976, and private organisations play a major role in this process.

Pre-vocational training activities for mentally retarded as well as deaf and blind children are provided in their respective schools.

General vocational training programmes are open to certain disabled persons. Deaf students, in particular, may attend courses provided in general training institutions, e.g. courses for industrial sewing-machine operators.

The Barbados Council provides co-ordination of activities and services and is in charge of improving the quality and delivery of services for disabled persons.

2. Employment

(a) Open employment

The Employment Exchange of the Ministry of Labour and Community Services was established in 1977 and provides vocational assessment counselling and selective placement services for the disabled.

Although no quota scheme exists, Public Services offer many employment opportunities to qualified disabled persons.

(b) Sheltered employment

The voluntary workshop for the blind and a psychiatric hospital provide sheltered employment facilities. In the former, workers specialise in crafts utilising local and imported straw. In the latter, patients are trained in shoe repairs, restoration of furniture, printing, gardening, etc.

3. Future plans

It has been proposed to include special provisions for the employment of the disabled in new factory legislation. It is also intended to establish special production workshops for the disabled.

BELGIUM

1. Legislative provisions

The Law concerning Social Resettlement of the Disabled (1963) provides for the establishment of a National Fund for the Social Resettlement of the Disabled (FNRSH), the terms of which are to guarantee or secure for the disabled a comprehensive and co-ordinated programme of social and vocational rehabilitation. The FNRSH comes under the responsibility of the Ministry of Employment and Labour and has a board of management supported by two technical committees (one social, the other medical).

2. Vocational rehabilitation services

The National Fund for the Social Resettlement of the Disabled (FNRSH) grants subsidies for the creation, alteration, extension and maintenance of approved vocational rehabilitation centres or services.

The different measures include:

- vocational guidance, which is provided in ordinary or specialised training institutions, in the training centres approved by the FNRSH or in those run by the National Employment Office (ONEM);

- vocational training, which is provided in general special programmes:

    (a) general programmes

        - ordinary training institutions are open to many disabled persons, provided that appropriate adaptations are made (e.g. accessibility to buildings assured); the disabled receive special allowances from the FNRSH for educational aids as well as for transportation;

        - vocational training centres (approved by FNRSH) offer programmes in business methods, handicrafts, gardening, etc.;

        - accelerated training or retraining courses offered in the training centres run by the National Employment Office (ONEM) for job applicants eligible for vocational training.

    (b) special programmes

        They include specialised centres for the disabled and a special apprenticeship scheme based on a contract between the employer and the disabled.

3.   Employment

The National Employment Office (ONEM) is responsible for the placement of disabled persons. Regional ONEM offices have specialised placement officers who try to locate posts which correspond best to the training ability and preference of the disabled.

(a)   Open employment

The law embodies the principle of an obligation to employ the disabled. For the private sector, the law lays down a proportion for each economic sector. Furthermore, undertakings which receive state financial help to expand their business must employ a certain number of disabled persons.

For the public sector, the proportion of disabled is determined by the Council of Ministers.

Employers are offered incentives to employ disabled persons such as financial assistance for workplace modifications and other additional expenses incurred by employing disabled workers.

(b)   Sheltered employment

The law provides for the placement of severely disabled persons in sheltered workshops set up or subsidised by the National Fund when such persons cannot be integrated into general employment. The workshops operate on the basis of subcontract work and most of them are incorporated in the form of non-profit-making associations.

Any disabled person who wishes to benefit from the above-mentioned services must be registered with the FNRSH.

4.   Research

An Association for Integration in Data Processing was created in 1975 to extend job opportunities in this field to handicapped people. The Association provides computer programmer's training for motor and visually handicapped persons. This experimental study is approved by the European Community and receives subsidies from the National Fund.

BOTSWANA

1.   Vocational_rehabilitation_services/employment

In the early 1970s the Government included the following clause in its National Development Plan (1973-78): "Insufficient attention has been paid to the special problems of handicapped persons ... It is the Government's intention to seek assistance in the preparation of a programme of detection, care, training and rehabilitation of disabled persons ...".

A National Council for the Handicapped was created in 1980 and acts as the over-all co-ordinating body in matters relating to the handicapped. As far as vocational rehabilitation is concerned, the Council advises and recommends the Government and non-governmental agencies on appropriate programmes and future plans. The Council is composed of representatives from the Government and voluntary agencies or associations dealing with handicapped persons.

At the present time, there are:

- two vocational rehabilitation centres for the physically handicapped, run by the Red Cross Society. They provide a one- to two-year programme of training to enable the disabled to find employemnt or set up their own workshops in their villages;

- one Rehabilitation Centre for the Blind open to blind persons between 10 and 49 years of age. Trainees are paid an allowance based on the sale of products of the workshop.

The centres employ approximately ten professionally trained social workers who work with handicapped persons either at the central level or in four different regions, performing the duties of a regional social welfare officer and providing counselling and guidance to the handicapped and their families.

A training programme was recently launched for field workers in the community. Its aim is to improve the physical, educational and vocational potentialities and independence of the disabled. Emphasis is placed on helping the family members to train their disabled. Family counsellors, teachers, voluntary organisations and social workers are involved in the programme.

2.   Research

An attempt has been made to identify and register disabled persons.

BRAZIL

1. Legislative provisions

    -   Orders No. SPS-20 (1975) and No. SPS-5 (1980) deal with
        vocational rehabilitation;

    -   Decree No. 77.077 (1976) is a consolidated text of the social
        welfare acts relating to vocational rehabilitation;

    -   Decree No. 83'080 (1979) provides for social welfare benefits
        concerning vocational rehabilitation.

Two further directives provide for co-ordination between vocational
rehabilitation, medical care and occupational accident policies.

Disabled persons entitled to vocational rehabilitation programmes
(see pt. 2) are defined as those whose working capacity has been
reduced through illness or accident at work and who are unable to
exercise their normal occupation or activity.

2. Vocational rehabilitation services

Under the legislative provisions, social welfare services are
available through the National Institute of Social Welfare (INPS)
which has so far established 18 vocational rehabilitation centres.
These are all located in the cities with the highest concentration
of disabled persons.

The programmes developed in these centres include medical, psychological and vocational assessment of the disabled as well as
placement, employment and follow-up services. They are carried out
by a multidisciplinary team including physician, social assistant,
psychologist, physiotherapist, occupational therapist, speech
therapist, instructor in trades and crafts, instructor in basic
education and a technician in orthotics and prosthetics.

BULGARIA

1. Legislative provisions

The rights and obligations of handicapped persons are defined within:

- the Bulgarian Constitution;

- the Labour Code (1951) [amended: 1957/1963/1968].

On this basis, the following legislative provisions have been adopted:

- Decree No. 77 (1951) [and its amendments] relating to social assistance. It provides for resettlement of disabled persons;

- Regulation No. 7 (1961) deals with the establishment of a network of vocational training institutions called "Troud" (see pt. 2.2);

- Decree No. 38 (1980) relates to the resettlement of handicapped people. It sets down the basic principles of vocational rehabilitation and specifies that workers (whether under regular contract or not) are eligible for resettlement if they are unable to perform their duties for more than 15 days for reason of sickness or work accident, provided they are capable of performing the same or similar work in different working conditions;

  the same decree (and its regulations) also provide for sheltered employment;

- Regulation No. 10 (1980) provides for special tax benefits to disabled persons.

2. Vocational rehabilitation services

    2.1 Organisation

At the national level, the Ministry of Public Health (in consultation with the Ministry of Internal Trade, the Central Bulgarian Trade Unions and other interested organisations) is empowered to co-ordinate all matters relating to vocational rehabilitation.

At the regional level, this task is entrusted to the committees of the district or urban people's council.

    2.2 Services

Vocational assessment and guidance services are provided by specialised committees, while vocational training is carried out either within the normal vocational schools or within the network of vocational rehabilitation institutions "Troud" (Work). They provide training or retraining to all disabled people according to the indications specified by industrial medical boards. An hourly allowance is provided to the disabled trainees during the training period.

3.   Employment

(a)   Reserved employment

All establishments and state organisations are required to reserve every year up to 10 per cent of all posts for handicapped people who have been vocationally rehabilitated and referred by the Industrial Medical Board.

According to the National Plan, up to 50 per cent of all posts in factories or undertakings could be selected for vocationally rehabilitated persons.

Handicapped workers who are re-employed receive a salary that corresponds to their productivity. If this is less than the disability allowance, the difference is covered by the social security scheme. Penalties are imposed in cases of non-compliance.

(b)   Sheltered employment

Sheltered employment is provided in the Invalids' Co-operatives. They are productive units within the co-operatives, concentrating on activities allocated to them by state authorities, e.g. hardware manufacture, bookbinding, assembly work, etc. They benefit from tax reductions and receive subsidies in order to adapt jobs and workplaces, thus making them accessible to severely handicapped persons.

Other sheltered enterprises have been established by the Union of the Blind and the Deaf.

BURMA

1. Vocational rehabilitation services

Whilst nò legislation concerning rehabilitation of the disabled has been enacted, the Department of Social Welfare and Co-operatives in the Ministry of Social Welfare is responsible for providing social rehabilitation services to the physically handicapped.

Blind adolescents and adults are entitled to vocational training in cane and bamboo work.

A vocational training centre for physically disabled adults provides training in carpentry, sewing, bookbinding, printing and repair of electrical appliances.

2. Employment

Upon completion of the training programmes, disabled persons may be employed in production co-operatives which have been established under the auspices of the Ministry of Social Welfare.

BURUNDI

1. Vocational rehabilitation services

There is no vocational rehabilitation centre as such, but some
training activities in sewing and shoemaking are carried out in
medical rehabilitation centres to prepare disabled persons for
integration into society.

2. Projects

The Government is currently planning short- and long-term vocational
training programmes for the disabled.

BYELORUSSIAN SOVIET SOCIALIST REPUBLIC

1.   Legislative provisions

The Byelorussian SSR Constitution grants basic rights to all citizens including disabled persons, such as the right to work and the right to health and protection. Other provisions are included in:

- the Byelorussian SSR Public Health Act (1970);

- the Byelorussian SSR Labour Code;

- the Byelorussian SSR National Education Act (1974).

2.   Vocational rehabilitation services

Work therapy, vocational training and retraining (the first level of the rehabilitation process) are available for the disabled through the network of state vocational-technical schools, special residential schools, secondary and higher educational establishments, as well as through on-the-job training.

3.   Employment

Resettlement in open employment and resettlement in special undertakings represent the second level of the rehabilitation process. Partially disabled persons are, whenever possible, given work suited to their state of health in the undertaking or establishment in which they worked before the onset of the disability.

The Byelorussian Soviet Socialist Republic ministries, departments and executive committees of the local Soviets of People's Deputies approve, for the undertakings within their jurisdiction, lists of occupations and posts in which working conditions are such that they can be effectively filled by disabled persons.

Specific measures have been taken for other groups of handicapped:

- persons suffering from tuberculosis, cardiovascular, nervous and mental diseases are trained and employed in special workshops or enclaves established within general undertakings;

- blind and deaf people are cared for by their respective societies which operate 26 research-production undertakings;

- severely disabled persons who need specialised and constant care are provided with opportunities for home work. Industrial undertakings supply them with material, tools and appliances. At present, there are nine home-work undertakings in operation and 44 branches and sections employing disabled homeworkers.

In general, disabled persons are granted shorter daily or weekly working hours and longer paid annual leave up to 24 working days.

4. Research

The Scientific Research Institute on the Resettlement and Organisation of Work for Disabled Persons (established in 1967) is
responsible for the study of problems relating to the vocational
rehabilitation and resettlement of the disabled. Research work is
carried out in the fields of industrial safety, improvement of
working conditions and labour protection as well as prevention of
disability.

UNITED REPUBLIC OF CAMEROON

1.   Vocational rehabilitation services

There are no legislative provisions for rehabilitation services.

Until the early 1960s, assistance to handicapped persons was limited to social and financial support to blind and physically handicapped persons.

Subsequently, basic vocational training activities have been developed and carried out in:

- a small public residential centre which provides training programmes in agriculture;

- a rehabilitation centre for the deaf-mute which offers speech training and vocational activities such as sewing, embroidery, craft work and clerical work.

Work accident victims are provided with rehabilitation programmes through the National Social Welfare Fund (CNPS).

In 1977, a Rehabilitation Section for Handicapped Persons was created in the new Ministry of Social Welfare. This section is a co-ordinating body for all activities run by public or private sectors in the rehabilitation field.

2.   Future plans

It is intended to conduct special statistical surveys on disability problems as well as information campaigns on the prevention of disability and development of specialised vocational training programmes.

CANADA

1. Legislative provisions

Vocational rehabilitation provisions have been adopted in the framework of the federal system as follows:

- federal legislation which authorises federal-provincial
  programmes;

- legislation which is exclusively federal;

- federal legislation which complements legislation at the
  provincial level (specially for prevention and protection).

On that basis, the following main provisions have been enacted:

- The Government Employees' Compensation Act (1918) and Merchant
  Seamen Compensation Act (1946): both Acts have important
  provisions for the rehabilitation of injured workers.

- The Department of National Health and Welfare Act (1944) which
  provides an information service on rehabilitation of
  physically, mentally and socially handicapped persons and
  establishes a Bureau of Rehabilitation to co-ordinate
  department initiatives in the prevention of disablement.
  Whilst legislation at the provincial level covers
  rehabilitation services, the Department is responsible for
  providing prosthetic and orthotic services to all physically
  disabled in Canada.

- The Blind Persons' Act (1951) and Disabled Persons' Act (1954)
  are integrated in the Canada Assistance Plan: therefore,
  programmes for the blind and the disabled are regulated by
  provinces and partially financed through federal plans.

- The Vocational Rehabilitation of Disabled Persons Act (1961)
  provides for agreements between federal and provincial
  governments under which the Federal Government contributes 50
  per cent of the costs incurred by a province in providing a
  "comprehensive programme for the vocational rehabilitation of
  disabled persons" (assessment, counselling, remedial services,
  information, training, etc.); the programme is administered by
  the Department of National Health and Welfare through the
  Social Service Programmes Branch.

  According to this Act, a disabled person is defined as anyone
  who, because of physical or mental impairment, is incapable of
  pursuing regularly any substantially gainful occupation.

  Some provinces also provide for the rehabilitation of
  different target groups such as drug addicts, alcoholics, or
  deal with specific diseases and disabilities such as
  tuberculosis (e.g. as in Manitoba).

- The Federal Canadian Human Rights Act (1960): one important
  provision of this legislation prohibits discrimination in
  employment because of a physical handicap. The Act also

encourages the development of measures to protect a handicapped person from discrimination in the provision of goods,
services, facilities and accommodation.

- The Canada Labour Code (1966) provides for occupational health
  and safety. Under this legislation, the Federal Government
  regulates such matters as fair employment practices, labour
  standards (minimum wages, safety of employees and industrial
  relations). More specifically, the legislation provides for
  the payment of wages at less than the minimum wage for
  handicapped workers. Similar legislation exists in the
  provinces.

- The Employment and Immigration Department and Commission Act,
  Part 1 (1977) and Adult Occupational Training Act (1967):
  under both provisions, the Canada Employment and Immigration
  Commission administers a manpower mobility programme to help
  underemployed, unemployed and disadvantaged workers to improve
  their labour market qualifications; these provisions also
  benefit the disabled.

In addition, all provinces have workers' compensation
legislation whose primary objectives are the rehabilitation of
injured workers.

Provincial legislation in Quebec has included mentally
handicapped in the group of legally protected disabled.

2. Vocational rehabilitation services

   2.1 Organisation

Vocational rehabilitation services are provided by the Federal
Government, the Provincial Governments and voluntary agencies
concerned with disabled persons.

(a) Federal level

The federal aspects of the programmes are administered by the
Department of National Health and Welfare, Rehabilitation
Services Division.

Under an agreement established by the law of 1961, the
Director-General of the Canada Assistance Plan provides
consultative and advisory services to the provinces in the
development and administration of the provincial programmes.

(b) Provincial level

In each province, there is a co-ordinator or a director of
rehabilitation who is responsible for co-ordination and
administration of vocational rehabilitation services.

(c) Voluntary agencies

Voluntary agencies at the national, provincial and local levels play an important role in the delivery of services to the deaf, the blind, mentally retarded and mentally ill persons, and contribute to the development of national rehabilitation policy.

2.2 Services

Services include assessment, counselling and vocational guidance, remedial and restoration services, information services, training services and referral for employment.

Whenever possible, training services are obtained from the Canada Employment and Immigration Commission (CEIC) under their Adult Occupational Training Programme. If an appropriate course for the client is not available through CEIC, specialised training is arranged by the province. It may involve individual tutoring, home instruction, correspondence courses, full- or part-time classes. It is carried out in special training centres, in commercial or industrial undertakings (on-the-job training), in private trade schools or even at universities.

Recently, the provinces and territories have made increased use of cost-sharing for services related to vocational rehabilitation programmes for individuals who are addicted to drugs and alcohol and for persons who have been suffering from mental illness.

3. Employment

(a) Open employment

Services for the placement of disabled individuals who are ready for employment are provided by the Canada Employment and Immigration Commission (CEIC) in co-operation with the provincial rehabilitation offices.

A number of programmes within the CEIC provide job opportunities for the severely disabled and other disadvantaged workers:

- the Local Employment Assistance Programme (LEAP) creates employment opportunities for persons who have difficulty in finding and keeping jobs. The programme functions with a great deal of flexibility and allows for the development of small businesses which are geared to the particular intellectual and physical capabilities of the participants. Learning how to make decisions and operate in a businesslike fashion, gaining experience, confidence and the necessary skills to compete in a broader job market are among the programmes' objectives. Thus, the disabled are provided with a broader range of learning experience than was possible in earlier types of vocationally-related training programmes;

- Outreach programmes provide disabled persons with a specific employment service. Thirty-three Outreach projects are currently operating. They are based on intensive efforts of

a counsellor in successfully placing a single client (usually
a person who had been given up as a hopeless case by numerous
other employment services).

(b)   Sheltered_employment

About 300 "activity centres" - or sheltered workshops - provide
marginal employment in assembly and manufacturing for the severely
disabled. Efforts have been made to increase contract work for such
workshops and improve product design and marketing procedures.

4.   Special_measures

Among the numerous projects to promote the employment of the
disabled, one has been particularly successful: organisations such
as the Coalition of Provincial Organisations of the Handicapped have
been given resources with which to hire staff to undertake a variety
of activities such as community development, self-help advocacy,
fund raising, public education and research. Most of these workers
are themselves young disabled people who are gaining valuable
working experience which may help lead to permanent full-time
employment.

CHILE

1. Legislative provisions

   - The Political Constitution of the State, Chapter II, provides that every individual has a right to a decent and socially useful job;

   - Act No. 10.383 (1952), Title I, par. VI, provides for services covering the risk of disability;

   - Act No. 16.744 (1968): Labour Accidents and Professional Diseases, Title V, par. 4, deals with services for invalidity;

     The Ministry of Public Health is currently reviewing this law in order to include the concept of vocational rehabilitation;

   - Act No. 17-238 (1969) provides for duty-free import of vehicles which will be driven and used by physically handicapped persons;

   - Decree Law No. 869 (1975) establishes a pension scheme for invalid persons;

   - Decree Law No. 2.25 (1978) provides for incentives for employers and grants for a specific group of handicapped.

2. Vocational rehabilitation services/employment

The Ministry of Public Health has at its disposal a Centre for Vocational Appraisal which assesses disabled persons' residual capabilities, schooling and work requirements.

The assessment is carried out by a multidisciplinary team composed of physicians specialising in rehabilitation, occupational therapists, social workers, psychologists and basic education teachers.

Employers of deaf-mute or blind persons are entitled to a bonus equivalent to 100 per cent of their obligatory contributions to the insurance institutions.

3. Special measures

Persons suffering from Hanssen's Disease are eligible for grants while they undergo treatment.

CONGO

1.   Legislative provisions

   -   Decree No. 7806 MJT/OGT (1976) provides for the resettlement
       of the disabled and work-injured in their former undertaking.

Labour legislation has general provisions regarding training and
employment of all workers.

2.   Vocational rehabilitation services

The existing rehabilitation centres provide vocational training
programmes.

   -   The Social Promotion Centre for adolescent and young
       handicapped women who suffer from poliomyelitis seeks to
       rehabilitate the patients and integrate them into socio-
       productive life.   The programme covers sewing and embroidery
       and is carried out in the form of a productive co-operative
       which is at present in an experimental stage;

   -   the institute for the deaf-mute, which offers training in
       woodwork and sewing, tries to find employment for the
       rehabilitees.

Both services receive subsidies from the Ministry of Health and
Social Welfare. A few other centres provide therapeutic programmes,
such as the service of a neuro-psychiatric hospital, which offers
work therapy to mentally handicapped persons.

3.   Employment

No quota scheme or job allocation programme has been adopted. The
promotion of employment is carried out by rehabilitation centres and
by social services in the Ministry of Health and Welfare which
provide follow-up services and encourage disabled persons to
establish their own professional associations (tailors, potters,
etc.).

4.   Research

Studies relating to training programmes for the deaf are currently
being conducted.

COSTA RICA

1. Legislative provisions

Act No. 5347 (1973) establishes the National Council for Rehabilitation and Special Education as a co-ordinating body.

2. Vocational rehabilitation services

The Costa Rican Social Security and the National Insurance Institute provide for the victims of work accidents and, recently, for indigents as well.

The Vocational Rehabilitation Institute was set up as a pilot centre in 1977; it has 300 places for physically and mentally disabled people. It provides for vocational rehabilitation, sheltered employment (100 people) and functions as a regional research and training centre for Latin American specialists. The Centre belongs to a private organisation; the Costa Rica Goodwill Industries Association but the programme is largely supported by the Government.

The National Institute of Apprenticeship (the official agency for training able-bodied adults) signed an agreement with the Vocational Rehabilitation Institute in 1978, which stipulated that all future technical, administrative and financial responsibility for the training of the disabled would be transferred to the Institute of Apprenticeship.

The same Institute for Apprenticeship has initiated and carried out a vocational training programme for the socially disabled (convicts, alcoholics and prostitutes), in co-ordination with the Vocational Rehabilitation Institute, the National Institute of Alcoholism and other institutions for the disabled.

Regarding staff training, two universities provide specialised courses to vocational rehabilitation personnel.

3. Employment

A Selective Placement Unit within the National Employment Service was created in 1976; it also provides follow-up services.

4. Special measures

The Government organises annually a Rehabilitation and Special Education Week to strengthen public support for services to disabled persons.

CYPRUS

1. Vocational rehabilitation services

Although no specific legislation has been adopted, the Ministry of Labour and Social Insurance established, in 1969, the Vocational Rehabilitation Centre which provides vocational assessment and training to disabled persons.

2. Employment

(a) Open employment

In principle, disabled persons have the same opportunities as non-disabled to perform work for which they are qualified and have full access to employment of their own choice.

A quota scheme has been adopted by the Council of Ministers under which 2 per cent of the workplaces in all government departments must be given to disabled persons.

(b) Sheltered employment

A Vocational Rehabilitation Centre offers production and sheltered workshop employment for the severely handicapped. The Ministry of Education runs other sheltered workshops set up in conjunction with the special schools for the blind, deaf and mentally retarded children.

3. Research

A special committee was appointed by the Ministry of Labour to study the problem of employment for the disabled and make recommendations regarding legislative provisions. The committee came to the conclusion that disabled persons with adequate vocational training generally succeed in retaining or finding employment. The committee therefore did not recommend the introduction of special legislation.

CZECHOSLOVAKIA

1. Legislative provisions

    - Act No. 121 (1973) on social security and its implementation;

    - Decree No. 128 (1975) of the Federal Ministry of Labour and Social Affairs. The law defines disabled persons as "those who, because of their long-term unfavourable health condition, are substantially handicapped as to their work potential";

    - Labour Code (art. 50/47/91) provides for special protection of the disabled against dismissal, special treatment in case of transfer and related employers' obligations;

    - Act No. 129 (1975) and Act 132 (1975) regulate regional responsibilities in the vocational rehabilitation field.

2. Vocational rehabilitation services

    2.1 Organisation

    Responsibility for the provision of rehabilitation services is shared by the following organs:

    - the Federal Ministry of Labour and Social Affairs implements government policy and legislation;

    - the regional Republic Labour Ministries are responsible for administration and development;

    - National Technical Committees apply specific rehabilitation decisions in collaboration with individual undertakings.

    Moreover, the local social security commissions are responsible for evaluations and proposals for rehabilitation and placement. A special consulting team advises on possible placement or suitable training for the disabled.

    2.2 Services

    Whenever possible, vocational rehabilitation services are integrated in normal training curricula.

    Vocational training programmes include formal instruction, apprenticeship training, in-plant training, etc.; when necessary, disabled persons follow programmes in special training institutions.

    The Ministry of Labour and Social Affairs is responsible for the training of rehabilitation personnel.

3.   Employment

(a)   Open employment

The great majority of disabled people are employed in regular
enterprises. The National Committees determine the specific numbers
of disabled people to be employed in particular enterprises and can
enforce such placements. Furthermore, employers are legally bound
to create suitable working opportunities, to adapt tools, set up
sheltered workshops and provide necessary training, etc.

(b)   Sheltered employment

Approximately 10 per cent of all disabled persons are employed in
sheltered workshops in the form of co-operatives run by the Union of
Disabled.   Economic advantages are given to co-operatives and
enterprises run by the Union.

4.   Research

Current research programmes are carried out in the field of partial
invalidity (prevention of disability and methods of rehabilitation).
Others deal with daily living problems of disabled persons.

DENMARK

1. Legislative_provisions

   - The Social Assistance Act No. 333 (1974) which became
     effective in 1976 deals (in its sections 30/42/91/93/95) with
     vocational rehabilitation and open or sheltered employment;

   - a Circular of the Ministry of Social Affairs (1975) provides
     for co-operation between social authorities;

   - a Circular of the Ministry of Social Affairs (1976) provides
     for a public employment service and reservations of special
     posts for the severely disabled;

   - a Circular of the Ministry of Social Affairs (1979) deals with
     institutions at the county level for severely handicapped
     persons (physical or mental).

2. Vocational_rehabilitation_services

   2.1 Organisation

Under the Social Assistance Act, responsibility for all services in
relation to retention, development and improvement of a disabled
person's work capacity has been transferred from Central Government
to local authorities.

The primary responsibility for guidance and counselling in
connection with the educational or employment problems of disabled
persons lies with the Social Welfare Centres of the local
authorities which may discharge this function by referring the
client to the vocational guidance officers of the public employment
service or to rehabilitation counsellors employed by the counties.
Local authorities have also at their disposal specially trained
counsellors who deal with the specific problems of various groups of
the severely handicapped (blind, deaf, etc.).

   2.2 Services

Vocational rehabilitation services are usually offered in ordinary
educational and training establishments with a view to integrating
or reintegrating disabled persons in the open labour market. For
that purpose, close co-operation between the social welfare commitee
and the public employment service has been established.

If disabled persons cannot benefit from services in ordinary
institutions, they are referred to special establishments, such as:

   - industrial clinics, which are set up to assess the capacity to
     work of the client and establish an appropriate vocational
     rehabilitation plan;

   - retraining institutions, which prepare clients for employment
     in the open labour market.

3.   Employment

(a)   Open employment

Self-employment is encouraged through financial assistance to enable
qualified disabled persons to start a trade or business.

The Ministry of Labour issues regulations on the preferential
employment of disabled persons in publicly regulated occupations.

(b)   Semi-sheltered and sheltered
       employment

Undertakings under public regulations offer sheltered employment.
Wage subsidies are granted to these employers under special rules of
the Social Assistance Act.

Disabled persons who are unable to obtain or retain employment in
the open labour market are placed in sheltered workshops set up as
small industrial establishments. Working co-operatives for the
disabled represent another form of sheltered employment.

4.   Research

Current studies concern pilot schemes in two counties under which
private employers are granted a subsidy towards meeting the cost of
offering sheltered employment to disabled workers. It is hoped that
the data will permit the formulation of general guidelines for the
granting of subsidies towards the establishment of sheltered
employment for the disabled in private undertakings.

DOMINICAN REPUBLIC

1. Legislative provisons

Act No. 116 (1980) and its Regulation No. 1894 (1980) established the National Institute for Vocational Training (INFOTEP). Under this new legislation the Institute will develop programmes for physically, mentally or socially handicapped workers, especially unemployed persons, prisoners in state prisons, juvenile delinquents in rehabilitation centres, as well as the disabled.

2. Vocational rehabilitation services

In 1974, an agreement was signed between the Secretary of State for Public Health and Social Insurance and the Dominican Rehabilitation Association (a private organisation) whereby the Association would develop rehabilitation services under state supervision.

The following services have subsequently been developed:

- a Physical and Rehabilitation Medical Service with eight operating units in the provinces;

- a Vocational Rehabilitation Service which runs nine different centres and a mixed farming establishment for training the physically and mentally handicapped in rural areas;

  both services are run by multidisciplinary teams (including physicians, occupational therapists, speech therapists, psychologists and social workers);

- a Special Education Unit for retarded children which provides, among other things, an Apprenticeship Therapy Programme.

3. Employment

There is an Employment Service which provides selective placement in private enterprises, co-operative groups or in a sheltered workshop run by the Association.

4. Special measures

Training, transportation, professional assistance and food are provided free of charge to the disabled persons.

ECUADOR

1. Legislative_provisions

    -   Presidential Decree No. 1327-A established the National
        Council for Vocational Rehabilitation and determined its main
        goals (co-ordination, planning, employment creation in both
        the public and private sector, etc.);

    -   Presidential Decree No. 1080-E provides for duty-free
        importation of motor vehicles for handicapped persons.

2. Vocational_rehabilitation_services

The National Council for Vocational Rehabilitation operates three
centres. Each of them has workshops for training in carpentry,
shoemaking, saddlemaking, mechanics, bookbinding, etc. After
successfully completing a 24-month period of training, the trainee
receives a "certificate of aptitude" awarded by the centre in co-
ordination with the National Service for Vocational Training.

3. Employment

Two sheltered workshops have been provided for severely disabled
persons. Here they are taught technical skills in binding,
wrapping, labelling or packing goods supplied under contract by
private enterprises. For some disabled persons, employment in such
workshops represents a step towards vocational rehabilitation and
social reintegration.

4. Future_plans

They include the establishment of co-operatives for the disabled in
both rural and urban areas.

EGYPT

1.   Legislative provisions

-   Act No. 92 (1959) and Act No. 63 (1964) authorises the Social
    Insurance Institute to support paramedical and vocational
    rehabilitation services;

-   Act No. 133 (1964) on social security requires the Ministry of
    Social Welfare to set up institutions for vocational
    rehabilitation;

-   Act No. 39 (1975) gives responsibility to the Ministry of
    Manpower and Vocational Training in the field of vocational
    rehabilitation and employment. A disabled person is defined
    as any person who, due to physical, mental or psychological
    deficiency or some congenital malformations, is unable to
    engage in a gainful activity. The law stresses that
    vocational measures are provided not only to citizens of the
    Arab Republic of Egypt but also to foreign residents under a
    clause of reciprocity.

2.   Vocational rehabilitation services

Sixty centres are run by the Ministry of Social Welfare and by
various voluntary associations for handicapped person (deaf, blind,
leprosy, tubercular and cancer patients).

On successful completion of a vocational rehabilitation programme,
the trainee receives a certificate.

The "Superior Council of the Handicapped" provides the necessary co-
ordination and planning.

3.   Employment

The Ministry of Manpower and Vocational Training deals with
registration and placement of the disabled in open or sheltered
employment.

A quota scheme of 5 per cent applies to each employer with more than
50 employees. The Ministry of Social Welfare, in agreement with the
Ministry of Manpower, may also reserve posts in the government
service exclusively for handicapped persons who have received
vocational rehabilitation certificates. Finally, priority for
employment and social welfare benefits must be given to the war
disabled.

The law includes a penalty clause for non-observance of the quota
law; funds thus collected are allocated to develop vocational
rehabilitation services.

EL SALVADOR

Legislative provisions

- The Constitution of El Salvador provides that:

  - the State shall undertake the support of persons without
    resources who by reason of age or physical or mental
    incapacity are incapable of work.

- The Social Security Institute, established under law, protects
  the insured worker against risks of disability from sickness,
  accident and occupational disease. The insured worker has a
  right to financial allowance, but the Institute must give
  priority in its benefits policy to rehabilitation.

- Decree No. 117 establishing Disability, Old-Age and Survivors'
  Insurance (1968) states that the Institute shall make
  available vocational rehabilitation services for disabled
  persons drawing pension and shall provide them with the
  prosthetic and orthopaedic appliances and other aids
  prescribed by the Technical Disability Commission. The same
  Institute must take the necessary steps to encourage
  pensioners in process of rehabilitation to follow appropriate
  courses of treatment.

  Persons receiving a temporary disability benefit are required
  to follow vocational rehabilitation courses.

ETHIOPIA

1.   Legislative provisions

Order No. 40, 1971, defined the status of the Rehabilitation Agency
for the Disabled, an autonomous public authority, which was
established to co-ordinate and supervise the activities of non-
governmental organisations concerned with the disabled (defined in
the order as "any person who because of limitations of normal
physical and mental health is unable to earn his livelihood and does
not have anyone to support him; any young person who is unable to
earn his livelihood must be included in the definition).

2.   Rehabilitation services

Rehabilitation services are carried out by national and local
government departments, as well as by voluntary organisations.
Sheltered workshops such as the Ethiopian Craft Centre, an umbrella
and dry-cell battery factory (United Abilities Company), and a rural
training centre offer various services, including pre-vocational
training, vocational assessment and job training. Because of
limited opportunities in the open labour market, Ethiopia has
adopted a sheltered employment approach for most disabled, extending
to both industry and agriculture.

4.   Future plans

Preliminary studies for the establishment of a regional rural
rehabilitation training centre and an agricultural rehabilitation
project have been made.

FIJI

1. Vocational rehabilitation services/employment

While there are no legislative provisions for rehabilitation
services, a Combined Council of Societies for the Handicapped was
established in 1971 to develop a national programme of Vocational
Rehabilitation Services. In 1979, the "Combined Council" was
replaced by the broader-based Fiji Rehabilitation Council.

The new Council has developed a small workshop where contract work
in packing, wrapping, labelling and addressing of envelopes is
carried out.

The Council also operates a sheltered workshop as well as a
production unit and a training programme which offer assessment and
job preparation services and employment outlets.

2. Future plans

A proposal was made that the Council should bring under its
responsibility the Orthotic and Prosthetic Clinic, which could make
useful equipment available for the existing vocational
rehabilitation programmes.

A new accident compensation law has been proposed. Under this law
a board would be established to assist those injured at work and in
road accidents; to establish liaison with industry, trade and other
organisations to promote safety and prevent accidents, injuries and
occupational diseases. A well-co-ordinated programme for medical
and vocational rehabilitation is to be elaborated by the board.

Finally, a comprehensive national scheme of vocational rehabilitation has been proposed, which would be realised with the support of
ministries already involved in the work as well as with the support
of employers and trade union organisations.

FINLAND

1. Legislative provisions

    -   The Care of Disabled Persons Act (No. 907/1946), as amended,
        is a central Act in the special legislation concerning the
        disabled. It provides mainly for vocational counselling and
        training services. All services are available to physically
        disabled, victims of chronic diseases, and (by Acts and
        Decrees of 1963 and 1965) to those disabled as a result of
        accidents or employment injury;

    -   the National Pensions Act (No. 347/1956) provides insured
        persons with medical care, vocational training and
        occupational counselling;

    -   the Sickness Insurance Act (No. 364/1963) and its relevant
        Decree (No. 473/1963) regulates rehabilitation within the
        scope of social insurance and determines the amount (2 per
        cent of the Sickness Insurance Fund) dedicated yearly to
        rehabilitation;

    -   the Decree on Sheltered Employment (No. 1073/1978);

    -   the Occupational Safety Act (No. 299/1958) and the Act on
        Occupational Health Care (No. 743/1978) deal with the
        maintenance of the working capacity of disabled people and
        those belonging to risk groups;

    -   under Ministry of Labour Decrees Nos. 401/1962 and 1121/1977,
        employment offices provide selected placement services to
        disabled persons.

Numerous legislative provisions deal with pensions for specific
groups (seamen, farmers, self-employed persons, etc.). Although
they do not formally provide for vocational rehabilitation, pension
institutions have voluntarily organised relevant services.

2. Vocational rehabilitation services

The underlying principle of vocational rehabilitation is the full
use of services and programmes established for the general
population, whenever possible.

Services to the disabled include:

    -   vocational guidance at the local and regional level;

    -   vocational training.

These services are usually provided in ordinary training centres;
disabled persons are admitted on the same basis as able-bodied
trainees. Increasingly, employers also provide specialised on-the-
job training.

Special centres have been established for the severely handicapped
who need particular attention during the training period. Although

some of these services are run by private organisations, they are
controlled and financed by the National Board of Vocational
Education.

3. Employment

Employment services for the disabled are integrated into the general
system of management services. The manpower authorities (Ministry
of Labour) co-operate with other authorities on such questions as
work assessment and adaptation of jobs.

(a) Open_employment

Disabled persons who have received training usually find appropriate
employment in the open labour market. A special allocation is made
annually in the state budget for the purpose of promoting employment
for disabled persons. Employers are also entitled to financial
support if they provide employment to disabled persons.

Disabled persons themselves are entitled to a disability allowance,
provided compensation from other sources (including remuneration
from work) does not exceed the amount of the allowance.

(b) Sheltered_employment

For the time being, arrangements for sheltered work depend on
voluntary measures of local communities and organisations
functioning under civil law. State subsidies are granted for such
activities. Sheltered employment is provided not only to physically
handicapped but also to mentally handicapped and mentally ill
persons.

4. Research

No comprehensive, co-ordinated research on rehabilitation measures
is currently being carried out. However, numerous institutions
(including university institutes of social medicine) carry on
studies and investigations, such as:

- follow-up study of persons who have participated in work
  assessment and rehabilitation examinations (Social Insurance
  Institution);

- research on factors that may impede or prevent the placement
  in employment and continuity of employment of the disabled
  (Ministry of Labour);

- studies relating to early rehabilitation as part of
  occupational safety and health care and the related
  development of vocational rehabilitation services at places of
  work (Rehabilitation Foundation Institute).

5. Future_plans

A revision of the provisions on sheltered employment is presently
under preparation.

FRANCE

1.   Legislative provisions

-   Act No. 57/1223 (1957) is a basic provision for vocational
    rehabilitation;

-   Act No. 57/1223 (1957) and Decree No. 79/54 (1979) deal with
    open employment for the disabled (priority and quota schemes);

-   Act No. 75/534 (1975) and Decree No. 74/478 (1976) cover
    vocational guidance. They regulate work assessment,
    orientation and resettlement as well as social welfare and
    financial social schemes;

-   Act No. 75/534 (1975) and Decrees Nos. 78/75 and 78/76 (1978)
    deal with economic problems of sheltered workshops;

-   Act No. 75/534 (1975) and Decree No. 77/1465 (1977) deal with
    wage guarantees for disabled persons.

All types of handicaps are covered by the legislative provisions.

2.   Vocational rehabilitation services

To ensure the development of rehabilitation measures on co-ordinated
lines with full involvement of the community and the disabled
themselves, an interministerial committee for training and
rehabilitation assisted by a national consultative council has been
established. The services include:

-   Vocational guidance

    The Technical Committee of Vocational Guidance and
    Resettlement, supported by a permanent secretariat and
    professional specialists (physicians, psychologists, social
    workers and placement officers), organises the services and
    selects individuals for training or retraining.

-   Vocational training

    The following programmes are provided:

    -   vocational retraining at specialised centres for the
        disabled;

    -   vocational training at an FPA (adult vocational training
        centre), i.e. at a normal centre, run by the AFPA
        (Association for the Vocational Training of Adults),
        operating under the authority of the Ministry of Labour;

    -   training contracts with employers;

    -   a training scheme in rural activities.

Training centres are established and operated both by the Government
and private organisations. The latter are affiliated to a
federation and receive public subsidies on establishment.

3.   Employment

The placement of disabled persons is the responsibility of the National Employment Agency, which has regional centres and offices throughout the country. The agency uses the services of placement officers whose task is to advise on the most suitable employment for disabled persons and follow up their progress.

(a)   Open employment

Certain jobs in the public sector are reserved for war disabled. Other disabled benefit from job reservations in the private sector.

Employers receive financial assistance for workplace adaptations and special training expenses (up to 80 per cent of the costs) and, under the quota scheme established by law, 10 per cent of the total labour force in organisations having ten employees or more must be disabled persons. This legal obligation may be partially suspended for employers who enter into a subcontracting operation with sheltered workshops, home-work distribution centres and other activity centres for disabled persons.

Vacancies may be filled by able-bodied persons only after notification to the National Employment Agency and after a 15-day period.

(b)   Sheltered employment

Available services exist mainly through three arrangements:

- sheltered workshops (mostly operated on the basis of subcontract work);

- workshops for occupational assistance (for the mentally handi-capped);

- distribution centres for work at home.

Sheltered employment is the responsibility of the Ministry of Labour, but most services are run by private associations and subsidised.

FEDERAL REPUBLIC OF GERMANY

Rehabilitation policy and services are regulated by a large number of laws and ordinances. They apply to a series of public agencies and organisations in the broad social security system, notably accident insurance, pension schemes, employment services, disabled veterans' grants and social assistance.

Legislation and regulations

- The principal law is the Severely Handicapped Persons Act (1979), as amended, which elaborates the provisions for the vocational rehabilitation and the social integration of disabled persons into the active life of the community;

- the law on the co-ordination of rehabilitation services (1974, 1980), as amended, assures equal availability of medical, vocational and social rehabilitation services as they are provided by different benefit systems of the various social security programmes;

- special ordinances (under the forementioned Severely Handicapped Persons Act) were adopted in 1980 to regulate the certification and organisation of workshops for the disabled;

- the Employment Promotion Law (1969, 1980), as amended, defines services of vocational evaluation, guidance, training, placement for all persons, and selective services for the disabled.

In addition to these particular and major laws, there are numerous other legislative provisions benefiting the disabled, which are contained in legislation on social assistance for war disabled, and on the administrative responsibilities of the Ministry of Labour and the Federal Institute of Labour.

Rehabilitation services

Persons are considered disabled who as a result of a physical, mental or emotional handicap suffer a diminution of at least 50 per cent in their earning capacity. Handicapped persons with a capacity loss of at least 30 per cent can be considered "severely disabled" if the handicap makes difficult their job placement or if an existing employment relationship is threatened because of it.

Vocational counselling

Local employment offices (under the Federal Institute of Labour) carry the main responsibility for vocational counselling. Special counsellors, with the support of professionals (physicians, psychologists, etc.) provide the services.

Vocational training and retraining

The central part of the rehabilitation process is aimed at assisting the disabled to obtain vocational qualifications; this includes apprenticeship training, pre-vocational and vocational training, retraining and advanced training.

A network of 21 vocational training centres (38 are envisaged) throughout the country offers approximately 10,000 training places (mostly residential) to young disabled persons who require initial job preparation. The centres also offer a comprehensive range of medical, counselling, social and placement services.

A parallel network of 21 vocational rehabilitation centres (offering some 12,000 mainly residential places) for disabled adults provides training, retraining courses and similarly related and supportive services.

The centres have a broad range of training programmes in the clerical, technical and industrial areas, as well as in horticulture and in service occupations.

All centres are governmental institutions that function in close collaboration with the Ministry of Labour, the Federal Institute of Labour and the organisation of the social security system.

Employment

Under the Severely Handicapped Persons Act, public and private employers having at least 16 workplaces must employ 6 per cent severely disabled persons. In cases of non-compliance, employers must pay a levy for each such workplace that is not manned by a disabled person. Funds so collected are used for the development of rehabilitation facilities and services.

Disabled persons can only be dismissed with the approval of governmental social service offices.

Employers who have already met their quota obligation and who create additional training and workplaces for the severely disabled can obtain substantial subsidies from the Federal Institute of Labour.

Workshops

A network of sheltered and production workshops offers employment opportunities to severely disabled persons who cannot function in the general labour market. These workshops must meet specified criteria of organisation, direct selection, programmes and services, and production sectors should correspond as far as possible to general industrial principles.

Severely handicapped persons' representatives

The law has detailed provisions on the election of disabled persons to works councils and other similar bodies to represent the interests and concerns of all disabled persons in the undertaking.

Research

Current studies deal with the development of new vocational training
programmes, cost benefit analyses of vocational rehabilitation and
in general a new analysis of the economic and social impact of
rehabilitation programmes.

Research has been proposed in the areas of integration of very
severely disabled persons, disability prevention and the creation of
supportive, humane work environments.

GHANA

1. Legislative provisions

The Labour Decree (1969, par. 23-24 (L1 632) deals with registration and placement of disabled persons.

2. Vocational rehabilitation services

Rehabilitation services are the responsibility of the Department of Social Welfare and Community Development which has a specific division for that purpose. Since 1962-63, the Department has been establishing vocational training centres for rural and industrial activities in all but one region in Ghana. With the exception of Somanya and Biriware regions, men and women are admitted equally to all centres. Skills taught in the various centres differ widely to suit the local needs. The duration of courses varies between 6 and 36 months.

Vocational rehabilitation involves the following steps:

- evaluation of the remaining potential of each trainee;

- vocational asssessment and job training;

- guidance and counselling for the entry (or re-entry) of the disabled into suitable employment.

3. Employment

(a) Open employment

Disabled persons compete for employment on the same terms and qualifications as able-bodied persons, taking into account the residual capacity for work, training and qualifications, whether in the public or the private sector. When seeking employment, a disabled person must first report to the Public Employment Centre. There he will be interviewed and registered by a disablement officer. The disablement unit will then provide selective placement services. All units are branches of the National Employment Service of the Labour Department.

A follow-up service is provided by a disablement resettlement officer who works closely with the agency or centre that was involved in training the disabled person. He is also responsible for informing employers on their social and legal responsibilities relating to employment and training of disabled workers.

A quota scheme has been introduced through statutory provision; under this scheme, each employer must have a quota of 1/2 per cent of disabled workers in his total labour force.

(b) <u>Sheltered employment</u>

Disabled persons who cannot be placed in open employment are referred to sheltered workshops or co-operative stores.

GREECE

- The Greek Constitution (article 21) stipulates that persons who suffer from an incurable illness, whether physical or mental, have the right to special services from the State;

- Act No. 963 (1979) on vocational resettlement of disabled persons provides for vocational guidance, training, placement and incentive schemes for employers who accept disabled workers.

In 1980, the Ministry of Labour and the Ministry of Social Welfare concluded an agreement of collaboration in the implementation of vocational rehabilitation services.

2.   Vocational rehabilitation services

Most services are provided by voluntary agencies but subsidised financially by the Ministry of Social Welfare.

Vocational training services are provided occasionally within the framework of similar services for the non-disabled.   This applies to:

- special training centres (under the control of the Ministry of Social Welfare);

- adult training centres (run by the Employment and Manpower Office (OAED));

- special units for accelerated training.

On-the-job training for disabled workers is given in many enterprises.

3.   Employment

Placement of disabled persons is provided through the normal employment services of the Employment and Manpower Office (OAED) with the support of a trained social worker.

(a)   Open employment

A quota scheme has been adopted for the placement of disabled persons in the public sector.   Employers in private sectors are encouraged to employ disabled persons through incentive schemes such as subsidies for job adaptation.

Trained disabled persons are financially assisted to start their own business (shoemaking, tailoring, dressmaking, knitting and other similar trades).

(b)   Sheltered_employment

Since 1969, sheltered employment has been expanded on a nation-wide
basis.   Sheltered workshops and a home-work scheme have been
established for the severely handicapped, including the blind and
mentally ill.

4.   Future_plans

A draft bill has been submitted to the Parliament concerning special
education, vocational rehabilitation, employment and social welfare
in favour of socially disabled persons.

GUATEMALA

1. Legislative provisions

   - Legislative Decree No. 295 (1946) established the Guatemalan Social Security Institute, which provides rehabilitation services;

   - the Constitution of Guatemala (1965) has a provision on the right to work; a formal vocational rehabilitation right provision is also included in social security laws;

   - Legislative Decree No. 17-72 established the Technical Institute for Vocational Training and Productivity (INTECAP);

   - Government Decree (1978 established a National Programme for the Vocational Rehabilitation of Disabled Persons.

2. Vocational rehabilitation services/employment

A short- and medium-term programme for the vocational rehabilitation of disabled persons has been adopted for the period 1979-82. The programme is primarily designed for the physically handicapped and focuses on vocational guidance, job training, and placement in gainful employment. Also follow-up services are provided.

The programme is conducted by the Technical Institute for Vocational Training and Productivity (INTECAP).

HUNGARY

1. ## Legislative provisions

   - A joint Decree of Ministries of Labour, Health and Finance (1969) gives employers the responsibility for vocational rehabilitation of disabled workers (adaptation of workplace, training and retraining and, if necessary, establishment of a special working unit);

   - a Decree of the Ministry of Finance provides for financial benefits to employers who make special efforts to employ disabled persons;

   - a Regulation issued by the Ministry of Finance (1980) provides for a flexible use of rehabilitation funds and a close co-operation between enterprises and administrative authorities.

2. ## Vocational rehabilitation services/employment

The labour sections in state and local Governments supervise and co-ordinate rehabilitation activities in enterprises. Sheltered workplaces and special workshops have been set up for workers who cannot be employed under normal factory conditions.

Since 1968, enterprises have been obliged to establish a Committee for Persons with Reduced Working Abilities which explores rehabilitation possibilities and makes recommendations to the management of the undertaking. The Committee includes representatives of the workers and management as well as the factory medical consultant. Each enterprise must keep suitable vacancies available for disabled persons.

3. ## Special measures

The Ministry of Labour and the National Council of Trade Unions have published guidelines on practical rehabilitation measures for enterprises and administrative authorities.

4. ## Research

Under the auspices of the Ministry of Labour and the Ministry of Health, several institutes of labour studies are carrying out research activities to modernise and develop rehabilitation services.

INDIA

1. Legislative provisions

    -   The Constitution of India provides that the State shall make
        effective provision for securing the rights to work, education
        and public assistance for the disabled and other groups of
        people;

    -   the Apprentices Act (1961) has special provisions for deaf,
        mute, blind and physically handicapped apprentices.

2. Vocational rehabilitation services

The Federal and State Governments are de facto implementing several
programmes for education, training and rehabilitation of the
physically handicapped in close co-operation with numerous voluntary
institutions.

Eleven vocational rehabilitation centres provide vocational training
to physically handicapped persons. Technical training and
university courses are offered by the Federal Government to the
physically handicapped who are able to reach that level.

Under the above-mentioned law, the physically disabled must
represent 3 per cent of the trainees in the Apprentice Training
Scheme.

Financial help is provided by the Central Government to teachers'
training centres for the blind and teachers' training colleges for
the deaf and mute, as well as voluntary organisations affording
training to teachers for the mentally retarded.

3. Employment

Action has been initiated to draw up new employment creation
programmes for the disabled. Employment co-operatives have been set
up by the Vocational Rehabilitation Centres to provide interim
employment to the physically handicapped until they obtain a regular
job in the open labour market.

As far as placement is concerned, 18 special employment exchanges
function in the country. Some of them have a special employment
officer who provides assistance to physically handicapped persons.

The Central Government must reserve 3 per cent of general category
jobs for the physically handicapped. The quota for public agencies
and oil companies is 10 per cent.

Tax concessions are granted to employers who employ disabled
persons. Other incentive measures have been adopted with regard to
sheltered employment, such as:

    -   loans at differential rates of interest to persons or institu-
        tions who plan to start up cottage or small-scale industries
        for the disabled; and

- concessions to workshops and industrial units towards placement of orders.

4. Special_measures

They include:

- fare concessions on rail, air or sea transportation and fuel subsidies on usage of motorised transport vehicles;

- free delivery of braille letters through surface mail and reduced rate for airmail.

5. Research

The Government has drawn up a scheme to sponsor and financially support research in rehabilitation of the disabled.

IRELAND

1. Legislative provisions

    The Health Act (1970) obliges the Health Board to provide
    medical and paramedical rehabilitation services to disabled
    persons. The Health Board may entrust other bodies - such as
    voluntary organisations - with that task.

2. Vocational rehabilitation services

    2.1 Organisation

The National Rehabilitation Board, a statutory body established by
the Minister of Health, has responsibility for the co-ordination of
voluntary bodies engaged in the provision of rehabilitation and
training services for disabled persons.

    2.2 Services

They include:

    - vocational assessment and guidance

       This service is available to those who have reasonable
       prospects of obtaining and retaining regular employment or who
       are considered suitable for training leading to regular
       employment. Vocational assessment is usually carried out by
       a medical officer of the Health Board in association with the
       placement officer or youth employment officer. Where more
       detailed assessment is necessary, this may be arranged by a
       special team provided by the Board;

    - vocational training

       Special training is provided to mentally and physically
       handicapped persons through the network of training centres
       run by the Rehabilitation Institute, a major national
       voluntary organisation.

       Training is given in a wide variety of industrial and
       commercial trades. When further training is required to
       achieve job placement, full use is made of other facilities
       such as AnCo (Industrial Training Authority) training centres,
       on-the-job training and vocational schools.

3. Employment

The National Rehabilitation Board operates a specialised placement
service and a youth employment service designed for handicapped
young people under the age of 18 years.

(a)   Open_employment

The primary aim is to arrange suitable open employment within the
area of the person's own choice. In 1977, the Government introduced
a 3 per cent quota scheme which has to be fulfilled within a five-
year period in the public sector.   It covers the physically and
mentally handicapped, provided they are capable of doing the job on
offer. The Government decided, at the same time, that a standing
interdepartmental committee should be set up (under the auspices of
the Minister of Labour) to monitor progress in relation to the quota
scheme.

(b)   Sheltered_employment

Sheltered workshops are established by the Rehabilitation Institute
for severely mentally and physically handicapped.

4.   Research/projects

The National Rehabilitation Board plans to:

   - carry out a survey of the progress achieved by mildly mentally
      handicapped persons placed in employment;

   - study the placement of the disabled in new kinds of industrial
      employment; in addition, the impact of microtechnology on the
      employment of the disabled will be assessed.

JAMAICA

1. Vocational rehabilitation services

Although Jamaica has no legal provision for vocational rehabilitation, a very broad programme has been established and is carried out
by the Ministry of Health and Social Security through the Council
for the Handicapped. The programme includes registration,
assessment, training and resettlement of the disabled. Four
different types of centres have been set up with the following
activities:

- an Assessment and Guidance Centre with workshops for wood and
  similar crafts;

- Production Workshops (one in an urban area, two in rural
  areas) specialising in garment-making, handicraft and toy
  production;

- Community-Oriented Rehabilitation Workshops offering woodwork,
  button-making, bamboo-work, etc., and also including a poultry
  farm;

- an Office Training Centre offering courses in typing, audio-
  typing, telephone operation, basic accounts, etc.

Voluntary associations still play a very active role in assessment,
vocational counselling and rehabilitation for the mentally
handicapped, the deaf and the blind. These associations operate
workshops with a large variety of activities corresponding to each
group's capabilities.

2. Employment

Placement in the open market has become increasingly difficult due
to the economic situation, the limited education of some of the
candidates for placement and the attitudes of potential employers.
Nevertheless, the country's policy is to integrate disabled persons
rather than to operate sheltered workshops.

3. Research

Research is currently being conducted into improving methods of
producing and marketing items from workshops for the disabled.

Other studies are planned: research in new technology and new
industries suited to disabled persons, a survey of all blind persons
and research into the prevention of mental deficiency.

4. Other plans

The Government plans to take special measures to develop barrier-
free environments.

JAPAN

1.   Legislative provisions

   -   The Workmen's Accident Compensation Insurance Law No. 5
       (1947);

   -   the Employment Security Law No. 141 (1947);

   -   the Law for the Welfare of Disabled Persons No. 283 (1949);

   -   the Law for the Welfare of Mentally Retarded Persons No. 378
       (1960);

   -   the Physically Handicapped Persons' Employment Promotion Law
       No. 123 (1963);

   -   the Employment Measures Law No. 132 (1966);

   -   the Vocational Training Law No. 64 (1969).

2.   Vocational rehabilitation services

On the basis of the above-mentioned legislation (in particular the
1969 Vocational Training Law), 17 training centres for the
physically handicapped have been established, which provide
vocational training courses adjusted to the needs of individual
disabled clients. At the national level, a vocational
rehabilitation centre and a comprehensive spinal cord impairment
centre have been established.

Specialised centres have been set up for the mentally retarded which
offer counselling, guidance, and adapted job training services.

Persons who become disabled through work accident or injury are
provided with facilities for medical treatment and vocational
rehabilitation.

3.   Employment

All physically or mentally handicapped job applicants are registered
and receive vocational guidance, on case work lines, from the time
of application until they take up employment. Responsibility for
these services rests with the Public Employment Security Office.
Thirty-eight Physically and Mentally Handicapped Persons' Employment
Centres have been established with a view to advising employers on
workplace management and adaptation of equipment; aptitude testing
and follow-up services are also provided to disabled workers.

For those who find difficulties in securing employment, industrial
units and sheltered workshops have been established.

A quota scheme which has been established requires that "all
employers must hire, as a minimum, the percentage of physically
disabled persons set by law" (this varies from 1.5 to 1.9 per cent.

The Secretary of Labour and the Chief of the Public Employment
Security Office have responsibility for controlling and supervising
the implementation of the quota scheme.

Employers failing to satisfy the statutory quota are required to pay
a monthly levy for each disabled person not employed in their quota
obligation. Funds thus collected are used to provide grants to
employers who exceed their quota and to those who make special
provision for employment of disabled workers. This is known as the
Levy and Grants System.

3.   Research

The Ministry of Labour undertook a survey in October 1978 on the
condition of employment of physically and mentally disabled persons
in 13,000 establishments with five or more regular workers. The
survey revealed some 233,000 persons with minor or severe physical
handicaps and 31,000 with mild or severe mental retardation holding
regular employment. Of these totals, 72 per cent were employed in
the manufacturing industry.

A study undertaken by the Ministry of Health and Welfare in 1980
revealed that there are 1,977,000 physically disabled persons (18
years of age and above) in Japan. This represents 24 per thousand
of the population compared with 18 per thousand when a similar study
was undertaken in 1970.

JORDAN

1. Vocational rehabilitation services

At present, some 10 per cent of disabled persons in the country benefit from the existing programmes carried out at pre-vocational training centres. Lack of qualified instructors and financial resources are among the main difficulties hindering expansion of services.

2. Future plans

Although there is no national legislation concerning the rights of disabled persons, the Ministry of Social Development has proposed to the Ministry of Labour that when the current labour law is amended it should include a new section on vocational rehabilitation of the disabled. This would provide for:

- the rights of the disabled to vocational training and employment;

- vocational assessment and guidance, vocational training, selective placement and sheltered employment services;

- special registers of disabled persons at employment offices;

- follow-up services;

- a quota scheme (3 per cent in undertakings with 30 employees or more);

- tax benefits for handicraft workshops employing at least 10 per cent disabled persons;

- financial assistance to disabled individual persons, co-operatives of the disabled and sheltered workshops.

LEBANON

1.   Legislative provisions

-    Act No. 11 (1973) provides for the establishment of a
     committee dealing with handicapped persons. This committee
     includes the Secretary of Labour (President), other government
     bodies interested in the problem and six delegates of
     voluntary organisations.

2.   Vocational rehabilitation services

The problem of the disabled is an acute one, especially because of
the present situation of the country, the lack of financial
resources and staff. The major rehabilitation services are   run by
private   and   voluntary organisations; the Government provides
financial assistance and co-ordination.

3.   Future plans

The Ministry of Education has presented a new law dealing with the
placement of physically handicapped persons in industrial undertakings.

Furthermore,sheltered workshops are planned and   new vocational
rehabilitation centres are to be created.

LIBYAN ARAB JAMAHIRIYA

1.   Legislative provisions

Law No. 3, 7 January 1981; Law on Disabled Persons. The law provides a variety of benefits for physically, mentally and psychologically impaired persons. These include special education, medical and vocational rehabilitation, employment and social services. The law also calls for appropriate domiciliary care whenever independent or family living is not possible. Grants under the Social Security Law are payable to the disabled person (or on his behalf) who cannot achieve successful rehabilitation.

2.   Vocational rehabilitation services

Vocational rehabilitation services are compulsory for disabled persons under the age of 40 but are available to older disabled persons who seem suitable for such services and wish to take advantage of them. Refusal to undergo rehabilitation may result in ineligibility for social security grants.

Disabled persons who successfully complete rehabilitation programmes are entitled to appropriate employment. Training diplomas and certificates issued by rehabilitation institutions are recognised as equivalent to other public certificates.

A special National Committee for Assistance and Care to disabled persons has been established. It is composed of representatives from all concerned government departments and other organisations serving the disabled. The committee functions under the supervision and chairmanship of the General Committee for Social Security.

3.   Future plans

It is planned that the special National Committee for Assistance and Care to disabled persons shall have its own expert staff and secretariat, which will carry out public education and research activities. The Committee will also be responsible for the strengthening of disability prevention measures.

MADAGASCAR

1.   Legislative provisions

Decree No. 69-145 (1969) (Social Insurance Code)   provides,
inter   alia, for cash benefits, rehabilitation services,
assistive devices and resettlement or retraining for work
accident victims.   Furthermore, the law provides for special
protection of disabled persons against dismissal by their
employers.

The principle of a quota scheme has been adopted and the Secretary
of Labour and Social Laws is entrusted with its implementation.

2.   Special measures

War-disabled and work-accident victims are entitled by law to
special privileges on public transport.

MALAWI

1. Legislative provisions

The Handicapped Persons' Act (No. 48/1971) provides for:

- the Council for the Handicapped (under the Ministry of Community Development and Social Welfare) which administers vocational rehabilitation services and advises the Minister on matters affecting training and employment of the disabled;

- the maintenance of a voluntary register of handicapped persons and the registration of associations whose objectives include the welfare of handicapped persons.

According to this Act, "handicapped" is defined as: "persons who, by reason of any defect or impairment of the mind, senses or body (congenital or acquired) are unable to take part in normal education, occupation and recreation, or require special assistance or training".

2. Vocational rehabilitation services/employment

Disabled persons are trained or employed in three centres:

- an agricultural training and evaluation centre for blind men. Upon completion of the programme, trainees are qualified for settlement in one of the agricultural development schemes or in their home areas;

- a weaving factory; and

- a small tie-dye centre.

Handicapped women and wives of blind farmers are provided with training courses in home economics.

These provisions cover only a small number of people with a specific handicap. Two area resettlement officers are available to assist other categories of disabled in seeking employment or in establishing independent activities. They work in consultation with social welfare and employment officers; they also operate the voluntary registration scheme.

3. Future plans

With a view to expanding rehabilitation and resettlement services, the following measures are planned:

- the establishment of a new rural rehabilitation centre;

- the development of workshops;

- the increase of professional staff of the Council in the three regions of the country.

A national survey is to be carried out in 1982 to identify the numbers of handicapped persons.

MALAYSIA

1.   Vocational rehabilitation services

     1.1   Organisation

Although the country has no specific legislative provisions, special
services for the disabled have been developed. They are run by
government bodies (Ministry of Welfare Services, Ministry of
Education and Ministry of Health) and by voluntary organisations.
While government services are co-ordinated by interministerial
committees, services of voluntary agencies are co-ordinated by the
Malaysian Council for Rehabilitation.

The Ministry of Welfare Services plays the major role in providing
field and institutional services for the disabled.

     1.2   Services

Institutional services are provided through:

-   a Vocational Rehabilitation Centre for the Orthopaedically
    Handicapped, established in 1965; it provides training courses
    in general industrial trades;

-   two training centres for the blind which have been established
    by voluntary association; one of them is in a rural area and
    provides training courses in agriculture;

-   centres for mentally retarded and spastic children which have
    been established by voluntary associations;

-   centres for deaf children established by the Ministry of
    Education.

2.   Employment

(a)   Open employment

Whenever possible, disabled persons are integrated into normal
socio-economic life through placement and follow-up services. Blind
trainees leaving the rural training centres are usually reintegrated
into their farming community.

Financial assistance, either by government bodies or by private
agencies, is provided to disabled persons who wish to start up their
own business. They may also receive technical and auxiliary aids
such as bicycles.

(b)   Sheltered employment

The Ministry of Welfare Services runs three sheltered workshops
which provide on-the-job training and emplcyment for those who
cannot be integrated into the open labour market.

A home-work scheme has been adopted with assistance from the Ministry of Welfare Services; homeworkers are provided with raw materials and help in marketing their finished products. Initially, the programme was intended for physically and mentally handicapped persons. It has been extended, however, to include socially handicapped persons who have problems in finding employment in the open labour market. The Ministry arranges for the training of newcomers to the programme, and also the retraining of those already participating, to improve their work quality and output.

3.   Special_measures

A system of registration of disabled people has been adopted.

4.   Future_plans

Under the current development programme, the Ministry of Social Welfare Services will establish one large rehabilitation centre for the physically handicapped and two more sheltered workshops.

MAURITIUS

1. Legislative provisions

    The Society for the Welfare of the Deaf Act (1968) and Welfare
    of the Blind and the Prevention of Blindness Society Ordinance
    (1947) provide that each Society shall establish and manage
    training centres;

    -   the Assistance Code (Code A/1971) provides for outdoor relief
        to severely handicapped children under 14 years of age;

    -   the National Pensions Act (1976) and Public Assistance
        Ordinance deal with pensions, allowances and financial support
        to disabled persons.

2. Vocational rehabilitation services

These are provided by the Government and by private organisations.

(a) Government

    -   The Ministry of Health administers workshops in hospitals,
        which provide patients with occupational therapy.

    -   The Ministry of Social Security is responsible for the
        Rehabilitation of the Disabled Pilot Project, designed to give
        training to young disabled persons in industrial trades and
        crafts. Upon completion of their programme, graduate trainees
        are integrated into workers' co-operatives.

        Under the project, disabled trainees receive a monthly
        allowance as an incentive measures.

    -   The Ministry of Education supplies teaching aids and teachers
        to the special schools for disabled youths; these are run by
        voluntary organisations which are supported by the Ministry of
        Social Security.

(b) Private organisations

These play an important role in the vocational rehabilitation
process. Special centres have been set up by these associations for
deaf, blind, mentally retarded and mentally ill children and young
adults.

In 1979, the Ministry of Social Security set up a National Council
for the Rehabilitation of the Disabled. The Council acts as a
central co-ordinating body between the activities of the Government
and voluntary agencies; it must also ensure that staff
qualifications measure up to an acceptable level.

3.   Employment

(a)   Open employment

The Ministry of Health has taken steps to give employment to some
physically   handicapped   persons   who   have   achieved   appropriate
training. Such jobs as, for example, packing assistants at the
central   supply   department   of   a   hospital,   orthopaedic appliance
makers (leather, wood, metal), seamstresses and carpenters at the
Ministry's carpentry workshop. Some blind persons work as telephone
operators.

(b)   Sheltered employment

A centre has been established for the blind and specialises in the
production of baskets.

4.   Future plans

The Ministry of Social Security plans to adopt legislation to
provide, among other things, for the inclusion of at least one
person in the Central Youth Employment Executive with special
responsibility for the employment of young disabled persons. Also
a general survey of disabled persons is to be carried out.

MEXICO

1. Legislative provisions

    -   The Mexican Constitution assures the right to a suitable and socially useful job;

    -   the Federal Labour Act (as amended 1973) deals with occupational injuries (Part IX);

    -   the Health Code (1973) and its executive regulations (1976) provide for disability prevention and rehabilitation;

    -   a special Decree (1977) establishes the so-called full-family development scheme (DIF) and a programme for the rehabilitation of handicapped children.

2. Vocational rehabilitation services

The system is based on social security and thus covers only insured persons.

Four Medical and Rehabilitation Units have been set up and another is to be opened in the near future.

The existing and future centres provide physical therapy, prosthetic and orthopaedic appliances, as well as general educational and vocational rehabilitation, including vocational guidance and assessment. The multipurpose workshops provide various job-training courses in such trades as electrical wiring, radio repairing, welding, etc.

Semi-literate trainees are taught to read and write during the training period.

Disabled persons who are not ready for open employment are sent to specialised training centres or to the social welfare centres of the Mexican Social Security Institute.

3. Employment

Employers are obliged to reinstate a newly disabled worker in his former job or assign him to other suitable work for which he has been trained.

Prevention of occupational injuries and diseases is the responsi-bility of the Ministry of Labour and Social Insurance (General Directorate of Occupational Medicine and Safety) in co-operation with other government bodies.

NETHERLANDS

1. Legislative provisions

- The Placement Act makes the local employment offices (working under the Directorate-General for Manpower/Ministry of Social Affairs) responsible for finding suitable employment for handicapped persons;

- the Disabled Persons Employment Act (1947) established a quota scheme of 2 per cent. It defined disabled persons as "those who as the result of mental or physical deficiencies, disabilities or disorders are materially incapable of earning a living by their work";

- the Social Employment Act (1967) made all local public authorities responsible for creating and maintaining suitable sheltered employment for all handicapped persons having need of it;

- the General Disablement Benefit Act (AAW/1976) and Disablement Insurance Act (WAO/1967) provide for disability insurance benefits; both Acts apply to the entire population between 18 and 65 years of age who are at least 25 per cent disabled.

2. Vocational rehabilitation services

Whenever possible, vocational counselling and vocational training are conducted within the facilities provided for all adults. Vocational training for disabled persons is carried out in:

- adult training centres;

- apprenticeship schemes;

- special establishments for physically and mentally handicapped.

3. Employment

(a) Open employment

Special consultants at local employment offices are responsible for finding suitable employment for handicapped persons. A variety of measures have been adopted or are being implemented to integrate handicapped persons into the working process to the fullest possible extent. For example: quota scheme, adaptation of jobs and of workplaces, part-time employment in sheltered workshops or in regular enterprises.

Wage subsidies are provided to employers who employ handicapped persons. The subsidy amounts to 60 per cent for 12 months and 30 per cent for the following 3 months. Moreover, employers of handicapped persons may, in certain cases, be exempted from paying the official minimum wage rates.

(b)   Sheltered_employment

Local authorities provide sheltered employment to handicapped persons who cannot work in the open labour market. Persons who experience difficulty in finding employment are also eligible.

4.   Research

Current and planned research programmes include:

- a study of the relationship between socio-economic factors and the increase in the number of disabled workers;

- an evaluation of two training centres;

- a study of referrals to sheltered employment and of the quality of work in sheltered workshops;

- the development of model procedures for enterprises in recruiting and employing partially disabled workers.

5.   Future_plans

The Placement of Partially Disabled Workers Act provides for a quota scheme of 2 per cent. The Act is currently being reviewed and the registration and control procedures will be improved through a tie-up with the social security system. It is expected that employment opportunities for disabled persons will be increased. Under the proposed new Act, which will apply both to the private sector and the Government, the quota will be raised to 5 per cent with employers having to pay a levy in respect of unoccupied quota places.

NEW ZEALAND

1. Legislative provisions

    -   The Accident Compensation Act (1972) empowers the Accident
        Compensation Commission to provide for vocational
        rehabilitation;

    -   the Disabled Persons Community Welfare Act (1975) requires the
        Director-General of Social Welfare to provide for pre-
        vocational and vocational training and operate a
        rehabilitation allowance scheme;

    -   the Labour Department Act (1954) provides for on-the-job
        training;

    -   the Disabled Persons Employment Protection Act (1960)
        authorises the Ministry of Labour to grant tax concessions and
        other advantages to sheltered workshops;

    -   the Industrial Relations Act (1973) provides for the payment
        to disabled workers of lower rates of pay than those
        established in the Minimum Wage Act (1945) and in the
        Agricultural Workers Act (1977).

2. Vocational rehabilitation services

The agency mainly responsible for administriation of vocational
rehabilitation is the Rehabilitation League of New Zealand (Inc.)

Most assessment and vocational training services are undertaken in
technical institutions or day-care centres. On-the-job training is
provided through agreements between the Department of Labour and the
respective employers. A special labour department training
programme preparing disabled persons for employment on equal terms
with other workers.

3. Employment

(a) Open employment

Selective placement is provided by employment officers. Twenty
positions outside regular staff ceiling limits have been made
available in government services for people with a mental handicap.
The Government also provides incentive measures to private employers
who employ disabled persons. Note: the Government has considered
introducing a quota scheme but has rejected the proposal on the
grounds of unsatisfactory experience in other countries.

(b) Sheltered employment

Voluntary organisations run most of the 70 sheltered workshops and
occupational programmes. This form of employment is actually being
extended.

4.   Special measures

Financial support is given to those disabled persons who require a motor vehicle in order to obtain or retain a job. Similar help is provided to disabled people who are employed only part time but who achieve a "substantial measure of financial independence".

5.   Research

Both governmental and private organisations have been undertaking various evaluative and statistical studies; one recent study by the Accident Compensation Commission is that of rehabilitation (including vocational rehabilitation) of patients with spinal cord injuries.

NORWAY

1. Legislative provisions

    -   The Act concerning Measures to Provide Employment (1947) and associated Regulations (1966) deal with employment services for persons who are restricted in their choice of occupation;

    -   the National Insurance Act (1966) provides for services and payments to handicapped persons, e.g. those in sheltered undertakings and special categories of disabled;

    -   the Social Assistance Act (1964) deals also with the financial aspects of vocational rehabilitation.

2. Vocational rehabilitation services

    2.1 Organisation

The Directorate of Labour of the Ministry of Local Government and Labour is responsible for rehabilitation policy and services. The Directorate's Board administers the services which include provisions for sheltered employment in public and private undertakings, disabled persons' co-operatives and in-plant on-the-job training. Employers' and workers' unions are represented on the Directorate's Board.

    2.2 Services

These include:

    -   vocational guidance in the schools and employment offices by vocational guidance officers and industrial psychologists;

    -   vocational training alongside the able-bodied as long as medical and educational conditions of the disabled permit. The Labour Directorate, in co-operation with the Ministry of Education, operates a large number of vocational training courses (supplementary, retraining, specialised training) which are open to and generally attended by handicapped persons;

    -   special work preparation for handicapped persons in vocational assessment and work preparation centres as well as in sheltered workshops;

    -   specialised training courses in rural activities.

3. Employment

The general employment offices provide specialised selective placement services to the disabled. Special counsellors provide assistance to the blind and the deaf and also to ex-prisoners. There is close collaboration between the various bodies responsible for some educational, medical and vocational rehabilitation.

(a)   Open employment

Whenever possible, disabled persons are placed in the open labour
market.   The employment service takes appropriate measures to adapt
- if necessary - jobs and working conditions to the disabled
persons' needs.   Disabled persons who have been trained in rural
activities are assisted to find employment either as farm workers or
on their own account.

(b)   Sheltered employment

Opportunities are available to all severely disabled persons, both
in public and private establishments and also in disabled persons'
co-operatives. A voluntary organisation for the blind operates a
home-work scheme.

4.   Research

The Directorate of Labour is represented in the steering group of a
research project under the auspices of the Norwegian Institute for
Adult Education. This is an action-oriented research programme
concerning in-plant rehabilitation.   Further studies on various
aspects of vocational rehabilitation are planned by the Ministry of
Local Government and Labour.

PAKISTAN

1. Legislative provisions

    The West Pakistan Employees' Social Security Ordinance (1965)
    has a special provision for industrial workers who become
    disabled in the course of employment; this covers medical
    care, injury benefit, disablement gratuity and a pension for
    partial or total disablement.

2. Vocational rehabilitation services

While there is not as yet any legislative or administrative
provision for rehabilitation services, vocational training for
disabled persons is provided by voluntary social welfare agencies.
Various associations serve the orthopaedically disabled, the deaf
and mute, the blind, the mentally retarded and patients suffering
from tuberculosis, leprosy, diabetes, etc.

Programmes cover a wide range of activities. For example, blind
people are trained in light industry, leatherwork, ceramics,
carpentry, etc. Blind women are given training in home economics.

3. Employment

Assistance in finding employment in the open labour market is
provided by voluntary agencies which run most of the sheltered
workshops.

4. Future plans

New vocational rehabilitation and training centres are to be set up
for the deaf-mute, orthopaedically disabled and mentally retarded.

A special project of the Ministry of Health and Social Welfare
concerns the adoption of a draft Ordinance for the Employment and
Rehabilitation of Handicapped Persons. This legislation will
provide for:

-   1 per cent quota for employment of the disabled in the private
    sector and government agencies;

-   establishment of a Federal Council for Rehabilitation of
    Disabled Persons with representatives of relevant government
    and non-governmental organisations to adopt a policy and
    implement the provisions of the Ordinance;

-   maintenance of registers of all disabled and handicapped
    persons by employment exchanges;

-   setting up of vocational training centres for the disabled on
    a national scale;

-   creation of a Disabled Persons' Rehabilitation Fund to receive
    levies from undertakings which fail to comply with the
    employment provision of the Ordinance.

PANAMA

1.   Legislative provisions

The National Constitution of Panama (1972) gives any disabled
individual the right to rehabilitation and social security
services;

-   the Decree Law No. 14 (1954) established the Social Security
    Fund which authorises and finances rehabilitation services for
    the disabled;

    the Law No. 53 (1951) [updated by Law No. 27/1961] establishes
    the Panamanian Institute of Special Rehabilitation (IPHE).
    This Institute is primarily devoted to the rehabilitation of
    young blind, deaf, mute, and mentally retarded persons. The
    Law also provides for a quota scheme of 1 per cent;

-   the Labour Code and Complementary Professional Risks Act
    (Cabinet Decree No. 252/1971) requires that employers retain
    or reinstate workers in their employment if they become
    disabled as a result of an occupational accident or injury; it
    also provides for the establishment of a national
    rehabilitation and readaptation centre through the Social
    Security Fund.

2.   Vocational rehabilitation services

(a)   The Social Security Fund has created the Medical Care and
      Rehabilitation Service which provides vocational
      rehabilitation and vocational guidance services. The services
      function in close co-operation with the Department of Economic
      Services (Vocational Guidance Service).

(b)   The Ministry of Health runs a hospital unit (Santo Tomas
      Hospital) which serves as a specialised vocational
      rehabilitation service for disabled persons.

      The National Psychiatric Hospital has two programmes for the
      vocational rehabilitation of mentally handicapped or mentally
      ill persons. These programmes include ergotherapy and a
      "partial hospital care" service for outpatients.

(c)   The Panamian Institute of Special Rehabilitation (IPHE) has
      developed a programme of vocational guidance and counselling
      for disabled persons.

3.   Employment

A voluntary organisation known as Goodwill Industries assists
physically and mentally handicapped persons who have received
vocational training to obtain employment. The organisation
collaborates with the Ministry of Labour and Social Welfare, the
IPHE and other private civic organisations.

By law, employers are obliged to reinstate a worker after an
occupational accident and must respect a quota scheme (1 per cent of

the workforce for 100 employees or more) for graduates of the Panamanian Institute for Special Rehabilitation. The same quota must be observed by the National Government.

No formal penalty clause is foreseen but the Management Board of the Institute is entitled to consider any non-compliance claim submitted by a disabled person.

4.   Future plans

The Government plans to collect statistical data on the incidence and distribution of disability.

The Panamanian Institute for Special Rehabilitation intends to set up a specialised employment service for the physically and mentally disabled, in co-operation with the National Directorate of Employment of the Ministry of Labour and Social Welfare.

PERU

1.   Legislative provisions

   - The Peruvian Political Constitution (1980) gives any person
      who is incapable of caring for himself/herself, as a result of
      physical or mental deficiency, a right to rehabilitation;

   - Decree Law No. 14560 (1963) underlines the right to work for
      any disabled person and charges the State and para-state
      bodies to provide employment for rehabilitated persons in
      suitable jobs;

   - Decree Law establishing the Office of the Assistant Director
      for the Promotion of Employment within the Ministry of Labour;

   - Ministerial Resolution (1977) setting up a Multisectoral
      Rehabilitation Committee (government bodies and private
      organisations).

2.   Vocational rehabilitation services

In 1979, the Ministry of Labour and the Social Security
Administration agreed on a pilot plan for the vocational
rehabilitation of the disabled. Its main purpose is to co-ordinate
action in vocational rehabilitation of persons who incurred work
accidents and occupational diseases.

The programme provides assessment and guidance services for the
disabled person and his family; vocational training; selective job
placement follow-up services; evaluation of training results and
labour market studies.

3.   Other measures

Tax exemption is provided, by a constitutional provision, to non-
profit agencies running services for the disabled.

4.   Research

A report providing information on the human and material resources
available within the public and private sectors was published by the
Multisectoral Rehabilitation Committee in 1978.

In 1980 the Governmental Directorate of Physical, Mental and Social
Rehabilitation Organs and Institutions in Peru was established to
undertake rehabilitation research.

PHILIPPINES

1. Legislative provisions

    -   The Philippines Constitution states that "every citizen has
        the duty to be engaged in gainful work to assure himself and
        his family a life worthy of human dignity";

    -   the Republic Act No. 1179 (1954) created the Office of
        Vocational Rehabilitation under the Social Welfare
        Administration (now the Ministry of Social Services and
        Development) to develop, administer and implement programmes
        of vocational rehabilitation and related services for the
        disabled;

    -   the Republic Act No. 2615 (1959) [amending Act No. 1179]
        established the National Council on Rehabilitation as a co-
        ordinating body as well as nine regional vocational training
        centres;

    -   the Republic Act No. 4564 (1965) authorised the Philippine
        Charity Office to hold annually one sweepstake to raise money
        for the Office of Vocational Rehabilitation of the Social
        Welfare Administration for the purpose of developing and
        expanding programmes for the physically disabled;

    -   the Republic Act No. 5416 (1968) [known as the Social Welfare
        Act] created a Department of Social Welfare and provided for
        the adminsitration of a national programme of vocational
        rehabilitation covering the socially handicapped, e.g.
        released prisoners, drug addicts, alcoholics, disadvantaged
        women, beggars and recovered leprosy patients. It also
        provided for a revolving fund for sheltered workshops;

    -   Presidential Decree No. 603 (1974) [known as the Child and
        Youth Welfare Code] provided for the rehabilitation of the
        mentally retarded, physically handicapped, emotionally
        disturbed and mentally ill children;

    -   Presidential Decree No. 1509 (1978) created the National
        Commission for Disabled Persons as a co-ordinating and
        consultative body to the President, and defined its
        objectives, e.g. adoption of an integrated and comprehensive
        long-term National Rehabilitation Plan; research activities;
        promotion of the active participation of handicapped persons
        in the rehabilitation process;

    -   Presidential Decree No. 1563 (1978) provides for the
        rehabilitation of infants, children and adult mendicants.

2. Vocational rehabilitation services

Under existing legislation, the Department of Social Welfare acts as
the Government's major arm in implementing an integrated and
comprehensive rehabilitation programme including vocational
counselling, vocational assessment, vocational training and
retraining, and the holding of seminars on rehabilitation.

3. Employment

A selective employment programme has been adopted which provides counselling and placement services in open and sheltered employment. Legislation provides for the employment of handicapped workers as apprentices or learners if their handicap does not significantly impede the performance of job functions. Employers are required to sign a wage agreement with the handicapped worker which must not be less than 75 per cent of the minimum wage.

Other protective measures for the handicapped workers have been adopted in the New Labour Code.

4. Special measures

The "Apolinario Mabini Rehabilitation Award" is granted to the Disabled Filipino of the Year, the Employer of the Year, the Disabled Groups of the Year, the Volunteer Rehabilitation Worker of the Year and the Professional Rehabilitation Action of the Year.

5. Research

The following subjects have been researched:

- survey of the personnel management association of the Philippines on the employment of handicapped and special groups (1978);

- follow-up study of graduates from the Vocational Rehabilitation Centre (1979);

- industrial survey and job analysis of specific jobs in manufacturing establishments (1980).

POLAND

1. Legislative provisions

    - The Planned Employment of the Disabled Act (issued by the
      Council of Ministers, 1967) lays down guidelines of vocational
      rehabilitation;

    - the Labour Code (1974) gives all disabled persons the right to
      employment and financial assistance;

    - the Council of Ministers Decision No. 281 (1973) deals with
      the development of invalids' co-operatives.

2. Vocational rehabilitation services

    2.1 Organisation

Since 1960, all vocational rehabilitation services have been
implemented, supervised and co-ordinated at the central level by the
Ministry of Health and Social Welfare, in particular by the Section
of Vocational Rehabilitation. Each administrative district has
Health and Social Welfare Services, with one or more specialists for
disabled persons. The services and specialised sections under them
deal with the planning of employment possibilities for the disabled,
the organisation of vocational guidance and training programmes, and
the control and supervision of actual work situations in which
disabled persons are placed.

    2.2 Services

Vocational guidance is provided in vocational rehabilitation centres
which are located in the districts' health centres.

Vocational training is provided either in normal technical colleges
or in undertakings where working conditions have been adapted. All
enterprises are committed to providing appropriate training to their
permanently disabled employees.

Deaf and blind persons are provided with specific programmes in
special training centres. The severely handicapped are entitled to
vocational training in co-operatives.

3. Employment

(a) Open employment

Upon completion of vocational rehabilitation programmes, and
whenever possible, efforts are made to place disabled persons in
establisments where they were previously employed; otherwise they
are directed to enterprises which offer a job suited to their
capacities. No quota scheme has been adopted, but employers are
required to hire the disabled whenever appropriate jobs are
available.

(b)   Sheltered_employment

Invalids'_co-operatives

This strong and important movement has gradually been developed and
expanded since the Second World War.   It now comprises 436 co-
operatives which represent a voluntary and autonomous association of
disabled persons.

The invalids' co-operatives, which benefit from state assistance in
the form of priority and monopoly production and tax concessions,
play a major role in providing vocational and social rehabilitation
as well as suitable jobs. They employ some 200,000 disabled persons
whose average earnings do not differ greatly from those of
industrial workers in other enterprises. Approximately 30 per cent
of the workforce in invalids' co-operatives are abled-bodied
workers.

Each co-operative must provide for the severely disabled (physically
or mentally) who, with continuing care and rehabilitation, can cope
with some of the production operations in the co-operatives.

Home-work_scheme

Invalids' co-operatives have set up home-work schemes for those
disabled who cannot work in co-operative workshops, either because
of severity of impairment, distance between home and workshop, or
other reasons. Homeworkers are provided with tools and materials
and benefit from similar social services as those employed in the
co-operatives.

4.   Research

Various projects are conducted by labour market authorities and at
university departments.   The Ministry of Labour has awarded grants
for study projects on employment prospects for physically
handicapped young persons and special adjustment measures for the
visually handicapped.

POPTUGAL

1. Legislative_provisions

    -   The Constitution of the Portuguese Republic, in its article
        71, requires the State to implement a national policy of
        disability prevention and treatment, rehabilitation and
        integration of the disabled in society;

    -   Act No. 2115 (1962) set up the National Insurance and
        Occupational Diseases Fund and provides for vocational
        rehabilitation;

    -   Act No. 2127 (1965) established a legal framework for actions
        in the case of work accidents and occupational diseases, and
        recognises the right of victims to rehabilitation and
        continued employment;

    -   the Decree Law No. 46872 (1968) established the Vocational
        Rehabilitation Service within the office of the Director-
        General of Labour. In 1969, this service was integrated into
        the Vocational Training Service and the National Employment
        Service;

    -   Act No. 6 (1971) is the legal basis for rehabilitation and
        social integration of the disabled;

    -   Decree Law No. 346 (1977) established the National Secretariat
        for Rehabilitation, which is responsible for a national policy
        of disability prevention and treatment, rehabilitation and
        integration of disabled persons;

    -   the Decree Law No. 519-A2 (1979) established the Employment
        and Vocational Training Institute.

Other legislative provisions deal with protective measures for
specific employment groups. In addition, collective labour
contracts have been drawn up which benefit the handicapped. For
example, the Collective Labour Contract for the Banking Sector
requires that at least 2 per cent of all places must be reserved for
the physically handicapped.

2. Vocational_rehabilitation_services

    -   The Ministry of Labour has the main responsibility for
        vocational rehabilitation and employment. Vocational training
        of disabled persons is conducted in assessment and vocational
        rehabilitation centres or, wherever possible, in vocational
        training centres for able-bodied persons;

    -   the Ministry of Social Affairs operates a rehabilitation
        centre (with sheltered workshops) for the physically
        handicapped;

    -   many private organisations and institutions are active in the
        rehabilitation field.

An agreement, signed between the Ministry of Justice and the Secretary of State for Population and Employment, has as its objective the promotion of vocational training for youths and adults from penitentiary establishments.

3. Employment

In 1979, a Rehabilitation Commission was set up under the Director-General of Employment, mainly as a co-ordinating body. It established employment centres, including sheltered workshops, for the disabled in two cities and employment offices for the disabled in the employment centres existing elsewhere throughout the country. By law, persons who become disabled during military service are given preference for certain public sector jobs.

4. Research/projects

A project is planned to study measures for an employment policy to help the disabled to obtain work in the open labour market. Moreover, four additional rehabilitation centres will be established and disabled co-operatives will be developed.

RWANDA

1.   Legislative provisions

Decree No. 17 (1976) provides for special education for
disabled students, especially visually and hearing impaired.

2.   Vocational rehabilitation services

A few vocational rehabilitation centres and two psychiatric institutions are run by voluntary associations and organisations. For the
physically disabled, emphasis is laid on developing particular
practical job opportunities, e.g. in welding, woodwork, bookkeeping,
radio repair, and clothes-making.

3.   Future plans

The Government plans to develop specific guidelines for communal
authorities on practical measures for the rehabilitation and
integration of disabled persons. A national committee is to be set
up to co-ordinate all ongoing rehabilitation activities.

SINGAPORE

1.   Vocational rehabilitation services

A rehabilitation section of the Ministry of Social Affairs provides
direct services to five categories of disabled persons: blind, deaf,
spastic, orthopaedically disabled and mentally retarded.

Vocational counselling and guidance are provided to disabled persons
to promote their integration into active socio-economic life.
Welfare services and family counselling centres are open to those
disabled who are unable to obtain regular employment.

2.   Vocational training and employment

The Employment Service of the Ministry of Labour has a special
training programme (known as the "Disabled Resettlement Scheme") to
assist disabled persons through on-the-job training in light
industrial   undertakings   or   through   formal   training   in
commercial/secretarial private schools. Disabled persons may also
qualify for subsistence, transportation and monthly pocket
allowances paid by their employer during the training period.   The
training programme is usually completed by job placement and follow-
up services.

SOMALIA

1.   Legislative provisions

There is no legislative provision for vocational rehabilitation.   A
quota scheme enacted in 1963 applies only to the private sector.

2.   Vocational rehabilitation services

A vocational rehabilitation centre for the disabled was established
in Mogadiscio in 1979 and is being developed with ILO assistance.

SPAIN

1. Legislative provisions

    Decree 2531 (1970) concerns the integration of disabled persons into employment. This legislation consolidated previous legislative provisions (Law [1963] and Decree [1966] on Social Security), which dealt with rehabilitation of disabled workers;

    the Decree provides for vocational rehabilitation, employment (including placement, protective measures) and financial assistance;

    entitlement to services extends to persons of working age, whose physical or mental capacity has diminished by 33 per cent or more and who, as a consequence, cannot obtain or keep suitable employment;

    the same Decree created the Social Service for Rehabilitation of Disabled Persons as a unit of the Directorate General of Social Security. Numerous legislative provisions have been adopted to operate in co-ordination with the new agency;

    -   Decree 1378 (1975) amended the provisions for employers' incentives;

    -   Decree 1567 (1976) established new requirements concerning sheltered workshops, job placement, social assistance for disabled in co-operatives, special enterprises and pilot centres;

    -   Act 36 (1978) regulated the administration of social security, health and employment services, and created the National Institute of Employemnt as well as a new National Social Service Administration both of which offer rehabilitation, social and employment services to disabled persons.

2. Vocational rehabilitation services

    2.1 Organisation

    Rehabilitation services are organised and run by various Ministries, especially Labour and Education, government agencies and by private organisations. They operate comprehensive services including training programmes, employment facilities and social security coverage for their members.

    2.2 Services

    Vocational assessment is carried out in provincial evaluation units where the degree of disablement is determined and appropriate measures for rehabilitation and future employment are recommended.

    Training programmes are based on Decree 2531 which regulates the utilisation of existing training facilities and co-operation with other organisations and agencies for the vocational training of disabled persons.

3. Employment

The National Institute of Employment provides a wide range of assistance to workers (including disabled workers) and employers.

By law, priority must be given to the disabled for certain jobs. A quota scheme has been adopted (2 per cent of the total labour force) for employers with 50 workers or more.

Tax reductions and financial assistance towards adaptation of work-places are granted to employers who engage disabled workers.

4. Special measures

Disabled persons who wish to benefit from legislative measures are required to register as disabled workers. The register is maintained by the Labour Exchange Offices.

SRI LANKA

1. Vocational rehabilitation services

Despite the absence of legislative provisions for rehabilitation, the physically handicapped, blind, deaf, mute and mentally retarded are entitled to follow rehabilitation programmes offered either by the Government and/or by voluntary associations which receive financial support from the Government. The services are organised as follows:

- the Social Services Department operates three vocational training institutions (for blind, deaf and blind and physically handicapped) which offer courses in a variety of trades such as typing, telephone operating, lift operating, clerical work, welding, beedi (local cigarette) rolling, etc.

  In addition to these three institutions, a sheltered workshop provides vocational training for the mentally handicapped; a new vocational training centre is being established.

2. Employment

The Social Services Department provides equipment and accessories for deaf and blind persons who have been trained in weaving and rattan work to help enable them to work at home. Finished products are purchased by the Department and sold at a retail outlet owned by the same Department.

Financial help is also provided by the Department to any disabled person who wishes to establish an independent economic activity. A rural rehabilitation scheme has also been conceived to prepare disabled persons to become independent farmers.

No quota scheme has been adopted, but the Government uses persuasive methods to encourage employment of the disabled. Directives have been sent to the heads of government departments and corporations. They specify that, notwithstanding the clause on physical fitness in the scheme of recruitment, vacancies should be filled by trained disabled persons, provided the candidate can discharge his/her duties satisfactorily in spite of the handicap.

3. Research/future plans

A national co-ordinating Council for Social Services is planning to prepare a job-oriented non-formal education programme for handi-capped youth.

SWEDEN

1. Legislative provisions

    -   The Security of Employment Act (1974) contains provisions for
        the protection of disabled workers against arbitrary
        dismissal; it places on employers the responsibility to find
        job openings for disabled persons that correspond to their
        capacities;

    -   the Promotion of Employment Act (1974) concerns elderly
        employees and employees with reduced work capacity. It
        provides for the tripartite involvement of employers, the
        employment service and trade unions in so-called Adjustment
        Groups in firms with more than 50 employees. The aim of such
        Groups is to advise and help disabled or injured workers to
        return to their former or a more suitable job with the same
        employer. As a last resort, clauses in the Act obliging
        employers to employ disabled persons can be invoked by local
        and national authorities (i.e. the County Labour Board and the
        National Labour Market Board);

    -   the Work Environment Act (and Regulations), 1979, provides,
        inter alia, for specific measures to be adopted by employers
        of handicapped workers regarding pay, work schedules and
        general working conditions. It also contains special
        provisions regarding the accessibility of buildings to
        handicapped persons who are defined as "persons whose ability
        to move about or find their way has deteriorated owing to old
        age, disability or illness, e.g. people who are blind,
        partially sighted, deaf or hard of hearing".

    -   a Government Bill (1978/1979) emphasises the universality of
        the right to work and declares that the aim must be for
        handicapped persons to be reintegrated in the regular labour
        market.

2. Vocational rehabilitation services

The Labour Market Administration directs special employability
assessment centres at which disabled jobseekers can be given
guidance and aptitude tests and provided with training
opportunities. Several other government departments and voluntary
associations are likewise involved in the provisions of
rehabilitation services.

Vocational rehabilitation programmes are also carried out in regular
training facilities or by private employers. In-plant training for
elderly and handicapped persons involves governmental financial
participation (75 per cent of wage costs for up to six months) which
can be increased in cases where the employer provides training to
severely disabled persons.

Finally, the National Research Institute is involved in the process
of assessment of work capacity and in the training of rehabilitation
personnel.

3. Employment

(a) Open employment

Handicapped persons who are unable to obtain employment can receive grants or loans to set up a business or trade on their own account. Employment in the open labour market is encouraged through different measures, such as financial assistance to employers for workplace adjustment and work assistants' costs. If necessary, employers may be ordered to increase the number of elderly and handicapped persons and, in extreme cases, to take on only employees referred to them or approved by the Employment Service.

Archive work for unemployed persons is also often made available to disabled people. Tasks can vary from general office work to professional research work and is managed by state authorities and public organisations. Persons employed under this scheme are paid under a special collective agreement.

(b) Semi-sheltered and sheltered employment

In addition to open or sheltered employment, a number of special semi-sheltered work arrangements can be provided to disabled persons, either in private or public enterprises or in workshops which provide an opportunity to improve working capacity and thus to increase the chances of obtaining work in the general labour market.

A home-work scheme is operated and has been specially adapted for severely physically handicapped persons; other specialised schemes have been organised for alcoholics and mentally handicapped. These latter projects include construction work, landscaping, forestry, etc. The National Labour Market Board also refers qualified handicapped workers to industrial work.

4. Special measures

Handicapped persons are provided with grants to meet the cost of a vehicle for travelling to and from work.

5. Research

The labour market authorities have special funds for research studies at the employment rehabilitation centres or in collaboration with university departments. The Ministry of Labour has awarded grants for projects concerned with employment prospects for physically handicapped young persons and experiments concerning special adjustment measures for the visually handicapped.

SWITZERLAND

1.   Legislative provisions

- The Federal Employment Act (1951) stipulates that employment offices are responsible for job placement of handicapped people;

- the Federal Disability Insurance Act (1959) is a major law which provides, among other things, for vocational rehabilitation services for disabled persons. Disability allowances are granted when vocational rehabilitation measures have totally or partially failed; amounts depend on the degree of disability. The Disability Insurance System subsidises both public and private institutions which provide the actual rehabilitation services for the handicapped;

  according to the Act, a disabled person is "any person whose earning capability is reduced permanently or over the long term through impairment of physical or mental health resulting from congenital infirmity, illness or accident";

- the Vocational Training Act (1978) regulates, inter alia, "basic training" for young adults who cannot follow regular programmes because of their low intellectual capacity;

- the Federal Employment Injury Act (1981) provides, among other things, for medical measures, auxiliary devices and allowances.

A special scheme - the Military Insurance Scheme - covers different measures in favour of persons who become disabled in military service.

2.   Vocational rehabilitation services

    2.1   Organisation

The Federal Office of Social Insurance supervises all rehabilitation measures which are provided through the Disability Insurance System. At present, the system is implemented throughout the country through:

(a)   104 compensation funds which cover both employers and workers and which receive contributions and pay allowances; each Swiss Canton has its own fund; the Federal Government has two funds and 76 funds have been created by employers' associations;

(b)   35 committees dealing with vocational rehabilitation measures to be provided to individual disabled persons. Each committee is composed of a doctor, a lawyer, a rehabilitation officer, a disablement resettlement officer and a social worker. One member at least must be a woman;

(c)   13 Regional Offices having specialised staff to provide for vocational guidance and job placement of the disabled;

(d)   one Central Compensation Office has responsibility for the control of compensation funds; this office also keeps a register of insured and handicapped persons receiving allowances.

As far as work accident insurance is concerned, a federal fund has been created for certain types of undertaking (listed in the law); private insurance must give the same protection to all other workers.

2.2   Services

Rehabilitation measures are carried out by a variety of organisations (public or private) which co-operate under special agreements with the Disability Insurance Scheme.

The services include:

- vocational guidance which is provided by specialised staff in clinics, in residential units or - in some cases - at the insured person's home;

- vocational training, which can be carried out either in schools, special centres or even universities. While in training, the disabled person receives a daily allowance which is higher than the disability allowance.

3.   Employment

(a)   Open employment

As far as possible, placement services are provided through the Disability Insurance Scheme. Employers receive grants for the adaptation of tools and workplaces. A large number of auxiliary aids are also provided (typewriters, dictaphones for the blind, wheelchairs, etc.) by the insurance system. Disabled persons who are able to set up their own business receive grant or loan assistance.

(b)   Sheltered employment

A great number of private and public organisations are involved in establishing and running sheltered workshops for disabled persons who are not able to hold a job in the open labour market.

4.   Special measures

In 1977, the Federal Council decided to encourage the integration of handicapped persons and ex-prisoners into public administrative services. The credits allocated for that purpose have been increased every year since.

In the Post, Telephone and Telegraph (PTT) enterprises, a special budget has been allocated for the employment of handicapped persons. Moreover, the PTT provides training to persons who because of disability cannot be employed or re-employed there) in order to facilitate their integration in other sectors of the open labour market.

TURKEY

1. Legislative provisions

    -   The Social Insurance Act (No. 506/1964) provides for
        obligatory vocational rehabilitation (before a disability
        pension is awarded);

    -   the Labour Act (No. 1475/1971) provides for a quota scheme;

    -   Regulations concerning employment of the disabled and ex-
        convicts deal with appropriate working condtions and job
        security. Since 1972, the Employment Service (under the
        Ministry of Labour) has been responsible for the
        implementation of these legal provisions.

2. Vocational rehabilitation services

Rehabilitation courses organised by the Ministry of Education and
the Directorate of Public Education are open to disabled persons;
special courses have been organised for disabled persons registered
with the Employment Service. The establishment of workers' training
and vocational training centres in Ankara and other provinces is
being prepared.

3. Employment

By law, priority and preference must be given to the resettlement of
disabled persons in the same undertaking. Furthermore, employers
must observe the following quota scheme:

    -   one disabled and one prisoner for every 50 employees in
        undertakings of 100 employees;

    -   two disabled and two prisoners for every 100 employees over
        and above the first 100.

In 1979, a Central Training and Vocational Rehabilitation Directorate was established to provide employment for disabled persons and
ex-convicts upon completion of their vocational training.

4. Research

The Training and Vocational Rehabilitation Directorate has:

    -   carried out studies on the skills of disabled persons between
        14 and 60 years of age;

    -   compiled qualitative and quantitative data (on disability, age
        and employment) regarding disabled persons who are registered
        with the Employment Service (July 1980).

UKRAINIAN SOVIET SOCIALIST REPUBLIC

1. **Legislative provisions**

   - The Ukrainian SSR Constitution outlines the general responsibility of government towards disabled persons;

   - the Labour Code provides mainly for preventive measures.

   The rehabilitation of invalids forms an integral part of the government health schemes, social welfare, education and the activities of state enterprises and establishments. The legal rights of disabled persons (physical or mental) are thus fully safeguarded.

2. **Vocational rehabilitation training/employment**

   Vocational, social and other rehabilitation services are carried out by the social security authorities at the district, municipal and regional levels, whereas the over-all co-ordination of rehabilitation services actions and management is the responsibility of the Soviet People's Representatives.

   Rehabilitation measures follow three basic lines:

   - medical rehabilitation and therapy;

   - vocational rehabilitation combining medical rehabilitation with vocational training or retraining;

   - social rehabilitation providing material support and assistance in daily living and working conditions for the disabled.

   The placement of disabled persons in productive work is based on the principle of the health safety measures at work and is carried out by a number of organisations, health authorities, trade unions, public organisations and social security authorities.

   Special vocational training and employment services are provided and run by the Ukrainian societies for the blind and the deaf. The authorities of the Republic offer a wide range of information sources as well as educational materialis to deaf and blind persons.

   Social services for the disabled are carried out by the social service branches of the district, municipal and regional Soviets of People's Representatives. The municipal and regional Soviets of People's Representatives also operate standing committees on health and social welfare which take care of matters involving social services for the handicapped and make recommendations. The social service branches of district Soviets of People's Representatives organise the work of the municipal and regional social service branches and provide, among other things, for practical assistance to enterprises and establishments.

3.   Special_measures

The war-disabled are entitled to special privileges and   allowances
in   connection   with   housing.   They also benefit from free
transportation in the city or in their administrative district.

Similar benefits regarding transportation are provided to other
groups of disabled.

UNION OF SOVIET SOCIALIST REPUBLICS

1. Legislative provisions

The Constitution of the USSR provides for a right to work and a right to free services to disabled citizens. Economic and social development plans of various ministries and departments contain special provisions for disabled persons.

2. Vocational rehabilitation services

2.1 Organisation

The services are provided by the State and form an integral part of the health service, social security, education system and activities of the state undertakings and establishments.

2.2 Services

In addition to medical and social rehabilitation, vocational training and retraining are provided at the worker's prior place of employment, through courses given under the general educational system, or in specialised state undertakings employing disabled persons. Training programmes may be given individually or in teams on a part-time or full-time basis.

For the severely disabled, vocational training is organised by a wide network of special establishments:

- auxiliary residential schools in the educational system;

- sanatoria of the public health system;

- residential centres belonging to the social security system;

- individual rehabilitation in rehabilitation centres, clinics and large hospitals.

While in training, the disabled have the same rights as all other able-bodied trainees and are fully maintained by the State.

3. Employment

Employment policy is carried out by enterprises, trade unions, public health authorities and public organisations. Social security organs are entrusted with the task of supervising and providing methodological assistance.

(a) Open employment

Each undertaking must provide employment to its manual and non-manual workers who have become disabled, either in the undertaking itself or - if the conditions do not allow it - in another enterprise, with the collaboration of the labour or social security organs.

A quota scheme (2 per cent of the total workforce) has been adopted.

Trade unions have special committees which supervise the resettlement of the disabled and compliance with arrangements made to improve their conditions of work and life.

(b)   Semi-sheltered and sheltered
       employment

Special undertakings and sheltered workshops are available for those disabled who cannot be employed in normal settings. There, they can find specially adapted working conditions and appropriate medical services.

These undertakings are authorised to apply up to 50 per cent of their profits to improvements of working conditions, social services and housing arrangements for their employees.

Home work

A home-work scheme for the severely handicapped has been adopted. The delivery of material, the supply of necessary equipment and the collection of the finished products are provided and organised by the undertakings. This relatively new form of work arrangement for the disabled is becoming more and more widespread in the USSR.

Training of scientific workers in the field of assessment of working abilities and placement of disabled persons is carried out by the Ministry of Social Welfare; training of qualified personnel and instructors is shared by various ministries and departments, especially those concerned with education and public health.

3.   Research/future plans

Scientific research on the prevention of disability, improvement of working conditions and allowances and development of rehabilitation services are among the projects elaborated by the Government to improve the actual rehabilitation system.

UNITED KINGDOM

1. Legislative provisions

    -   The Disabled Persons (Employment) Act (1944) contains
        provisions for the registration of disabled persons, an
        employment quota scheme, reservation of jobs and provisions
        for sheltered workshops. Furthermore, it provides for the
        establishment of a National Advisory Council on Employment of
        Disabled Persons (NACEDP) and local committees to advise and
        assist the Secretary of State and the Manpower Services
        Commission (MSC) in matters relating to the employment of the
        disabled;

    -   the Disabled Persons (Employment) Act (1958) makes two minor
        changes in registration for the disabled and reduces the
        minimum age for employment, rehabilitation and vocational
        training courses to those over compulsory school age, so that
        there should be no possibility of a gap between leaving school
        and any rehabilitation or training course which may be
        desirable;

    -   the Chronically Sick and Disabled Persons Act (1970) requires
        the NACEDP to advise the Secretary of State on the training of
        personnel concerned with the placement or the training of
        disabled persons;

        the Act also requires the Central Youth Employment Executive
        to appoint at least one person with special responsibility for
        the employment of young disabled persons and stresses the
        desirability of including on the National Youth Employment
        Council and the Advisory Committees on Youth Employment
        (Scotland and Wales) one or more persons with experience of
        work among young disabled;

    -   the Employment and Training Act (1973) provides for the
        establishment of the Manpower Services Commission (MSC) which
        has the power to provide employment and training services and
        employment rehabilitation services. The MSC is directly
        responsible to the Secretary of Employment and has three
        operating divisions: the Employment Service Agency (ESA), the
        Training Services Agency (TSA) and the Special Programmes
        Agency (SPA);

    -   Regulations under the 1980 Companies Act oblige companies with
        more then 250 employees to report on their policies for the
        employment of disabled persons.

2. Vocational rehabilitation services

Many services for disabled people are run by the Manpower Services
Commission (MSC):

    -   Vocational guidance

        Apart from the responsibilities placed on the MSC, all local
        Education Authorities are required by law to provide
        vocational guidance services for those attending educational
        institutions and employment for those leaving them.

- <u>Rehabilitation facilities</u> are organised through 29 Employment Rehabilitation Centres (ERCs) where opportunities are provided for disabled persons to adjust gradually to normal working conditions and to be assessed and guided as to the type of work for which they are best suited.

- <u>Vocational training services</u> are provided or sponsored by the Training Services Division (TSD). Their aim is to provide a flexible response to each individual's training needs leading to resettlement into open employment. The majority of disabled people receive training alongside the able-bodied in the TSD's skill centres, educational centres and employers' premises under the Training Opportunities Scheme (TOPS); the latter scheme offers a wide variety of semi-skilled training in areas such as automotive skills, business administration, commercial and secretarial work, craft and technical courses, engineering, electronics and computer programming.

  For more severely disabled persons, the TSD supports facilities at four residential training colleges run by voluntary bodies.

  Other training facilities are available. For example, under the Individual Training Throughout with an Employer scheme (ITTWE) disabled people may be sponsored to train with an employer on the understanding that employment will be offered on the successful completion of training.

  Finally, special training facilities are available for the deaf and the visually handicapped. They are run by voluntary agencies and sponsored by the TSD.

3. <u>Employment</u>

(a) <u>Open employment</u>

Disablement Resettlement Services have been established, in which the central figure is the Disablement Resettlement Officer (DRO). Blind persons are provided with the services of a DRO specially trained to cope with the resettlement problems of the visually impaired.

A quota scheme (at present 3 per cent) has to be observed by employers of 20 or more workers. By law, certain jobs must be reserved for the disabled. So far, car-park attendants and passenger electric lift attendants are the only jobs designated.

Disablement Resettlement Services may provide the following incentive measures to employers:

- grants towards the cost of adaptation of premises and equipment used by disabled persons;

- financial assistance for a "job trial" provided to a disabled person.

Furthermore, the severely disabled can also be provided with financial assistance to establish an independent trade or business.

(b)   Semi-sheltered and sheltered
       employment

The Manpower Services Commission (MSC) co-ordinates and subsidises
the provision of sheltered employment. The main provider of
sheltered employment for the severely disabled is Remploy Ltd., a
company set up by the Government in 1946 to give meaningful work
opportunities to severely disabled persons. It provides employment
to 8,200 severely disabled in 89 factories. In addition, more than
5,000 jobs are provided by the 128 workshops run by local
authorities and voluntary bodies.

Recently, Sheltered Industrial Groups have been created. They offer
the opportunity for small groups of severely disabled people to work
under special supervision in an industrial or commercial
environment.

A special service of the MSC assists sheltered workshops to obtain
contracts from central and local government and offers advice in so
far as equipment, methods and planning are concerned.

4.   Special measures

In 1979, a major national promotional campaign (the Fit-to-Work
Campaign) was launched to encourage employers to provide more and
better opportunities for disabled persons. An important element is
the involvement of management and unions. An Annual Award Scheme
for firms who do most to help the disabled has been introduced. In
1980, 100 employers won awards.

5.   Research

The Manpower Services Commission (MSC) is undertaking or planning
research in the following areas:

-   Rehabilitation

    In 1976, the MSC established an Employment Rehabilitation
    Research Centre. By 1980, the Research Centre had completed
    studies involving, among others:

        -   a survey of client characteristics in Employment
            Rehabilitation Centres (ERCs);

        -   assessments of the role of social workers and remedial
            gymnasts in ERCs;

        -   development of a Job Search Module.

Further studies (including the rehabilitation of mentally disabled
persons) are planned.

-   Training

    Research includes studies on access to training of trainees
    classified as suffering from psychiatric disorders and
    epilepsy; also evaluation of the TSD's Individual Training
    Throughout with an Employer scheme.

- <u>Employment</u>

   An examination has begun of the current arrangements for liaison between those responsible for rehabilitation of the handicapped.

UNITED STATES

1. Legislative provisions

Legislative provisions for services to the disabled go back many years. Early examples are:

- the Federal Employees' Compensation Act (1916), which provides a system whereby the Federal Government compensates its employees and their dependants in cases of work accident or injury; and

- the Longshoremen's and Harbor Workers' Compensation Act (1927), which provides for vocational rehabilitation of this group of workers.

Other examples of early legislation are:

- the Wagner-Peyser Act (1933, amended 1954), which requires the local employment service office to designate at least one staff member responsible for helping severely handicapped individuals to locate training resources and/or suitable employment. Applicants are considered handicapped if they have physical, mental or emotional impairments that constitute an obstacle to their employment. Alcohol and drug abusers are included;

- the Fair Labour Standards Act (1938, amended 1966/1977), which authorises the Secretary of Labor to regulate employment of handicapped workers at wage rates below the statutory minimum. The aim is to "prevent curtailment of employment opportunities" for handicapped workers in competitive industry, in sheltered workshops and for patient/workers in hospitals and institutions;

  according to this law, handicapped workers are those "whose earning or productive capacity is impaired by age or physical or mental deficiency or injury";

- the Wagner-O'Day Act (1938), which originally authorised purchase from workshops for the blind. Amendments to the Act in 1971 extended the authority to workshops for other severely handicapped persons, defined as: "an individual or class of individuals under a physical or mental disability, other than blindness, which ... constitutes a substantial handicap to employment and is of such a nature as to prevent the individual under such disability from currently engaging in normal competitive employment";

- the Randolph Sheppard Act (1938), as amended (1974), authorises a programme designed to provide gainful employment for blind individuals operating vending facilities on federal property;

- the Small Business Act (1953), which establishes two loan programmes: one for non-profit sheltered workshops and another for handicapped persons who wish to start up or operate their own small business.

Since 1960, there has been a considerable increase in federal legislation benefiting handicapped persons. These laws cover various
areas, but those which are concerned with vocational rehabilitation
are mainly:

- the Vocational Education Act (1963), which authorises a
  programme of grants-in-aid to the States in order to expand
  and improve vocational educational services. In addition, it
  requires a percentage of funds to be used to provide
  vocational education services to handicapped individuals.
  This is to allow handicapped persons to participate in regular
  vocational education programmes instead of placing them in
  segregated vocational classes. For purposes of this Act, the
  term "handicapped persons" is defined as: "persons who are
  mentally retarded, hard of hearing, deaf, speech impaired,
  visually handicapped, seriously emotionally disturbed,
  crippled, or other health-impaired persons who by reason
  thereof require special education and related services, and
  who, because of their handicapping condition, cannot succeed
  in the regular vocational education programme without special
  education assistance or who require a modified vocational
  education programme";

- the Rehabilitation Act (1973), as amended, places a new
  emphasis on expanding services to severely disabled. It also:

  - provides a statutory basis for the Rehabilitation
    Services Administration;

  - established (1978 amendment) a National Institute of
    Handicapped Research (as a separate administrative
    entity within the Department of Education). This
    Institute is responsible for research programmes as well
    as training rehabilitation personnel and researchers;

  - established (1978 amendment) a National Council on the
    Handicapped. Council members are appointed by the
    President to represent consumers, national
    organisations, service providers and administrators,
    researchers, and business and labour groups. It must
    include at least five handicapped persons, their parents
    or guardians;

  according to the law, "handicapped individual" means "any
  individual (1) who has a physical or mental disability which
  for such individual constitutes or results in a substantial
  handicap to employment, and (2) can reasonably be expected to
  benefit in terms of employment ability from vocational
  rehabilitation services";

  "severe handicap" means a "disability which requires multiple
  services over an extended period of time and results from
  amputation, blindness, cerebral palsy, cystic fibrosis,
  deafness, heart diseases, hemiplegia, mental retardation,
  mental illnesss, multiple sclerosis, muscular dystrophy,
  neurological disorders (including stroke and epilepsy),
  paraplegia, quadriplegia and other spinal cord conditions,
  renal failure, respiratory or pulmonary disfunction, and any
  other disability specified in regulations";

the Rehabilitation Act provides for a wide range of measures such as: flexible work arrangements, barrier removal, non-discriminatory measures, and affirmative action programmes (applying to government contractors and subcontractors);

- the Comprehensive Employment and Training Act (CETA) (1973) consolidated federally-funded employment and training programmes. It is directed to serve economically disadvantaged and unemployed persons. Handicapped persons are eligible to participate in most CETA programmes (1978 amendment). "Economically disadvantaged" and "unemployed" persons are defined by the Act "to include handicapped persons living at home or in an institution or receiving services in a sheltered workshop, prison, hosptial or similar community of institutional care facility";

- the Rehabilitation Comprehensive Services and Developmental Disabilities Act (1978) provides for specific programmes in favour of developmentally disabled persons who are, inter alia, persons who suffer from a severe, chronic disability which:

    - is attributable to a mental or physical impairment or combination of mental and physical impairments;

    - is manifested before the person attains the age of 22;

    - is likely to continue indefinitely.

Finally, a major advance has come through new legislation which protects disabled persons against discrimination. Such protection is included in the forementioned Rehabilitation Act (1973) and in the Education of the Handicapped Act (1974/1975 amendments), which provides that all disabled are qualified for federal grants. Furthermore:

- the Civil Rights Commission Act Amendments of 1978 expanded the jurisdiction of the Civil Rights Commission to include protection against discrimination on the basis of handicap;

- the Legal Services Corporation Act Amendments (1977) added handicapped persons to the list of clients eligible for services; and

    since 1980, the Justice Department is empowered to initiate civil suits against States to protect the rights of mentally retarded and other institutionalised individuals.

2. Vocational rehabilitation services

Physically and mentally disabled citizens are served through programmes supported by the Rehabilitation Services Administration (RSA), which is currently under the Office of Special Education and Rehabilitation Services within the US Department of Education. This Office, headed by an Assistant Secretary, has become the focal point in the Federal Government for matters relating to disability.

RSA and its (50) state counterparts, the state rehabilitation agencies, work jointly with non-profit organisations in solving the inter-related problems of the disabled in the community. Under the basic support programme, the Rehabilitation Act provides for federal financial assistance to States. Funds are allocated on a matching basis of approximately 80 per cent federal and 20 per cent States.

There are ten federal regional offices. Each has a Regional Rehabilitation Director and an Assistant Regional Director for the Office of Social Education and Rehabilitation Services. Every State has a vocational rehabilitation agency which has to submit every year to the Federal Government a full report on plans, policies and methods to be followed in expanding and improving services to handicapped individuals with the most severe handicap.

The state-federal vocational rehabilitation programmes include a wide range of services:

- counselling services, which are regarded as the core of the entire rehabilitation process. Counsellor and client work together on an individualised written rehabilitation plan. The Councsellor provides the guidance to assure that all necessary services are provided under that plan;

- training services, which include:

  - training with a view towards career advancement;

  - training in occupational skills;

  - related services, such as work evaluation, work testing and provision of occupational tools and equipment required by the individual to engage in such training.

Other provisions are included in the Vocational Education Act and in the Comprehensive Employment and Training Act. Payment of a weekly allowance to indivduals receiving training and related services is provided by the Rehabilitation Act.

3. **Employment**

The US Employment Service of the Employment and Training Administration, Department of Labor, was established in 1933 to promote, develop and maintain a national system of employment offices for persons who are legally qualified to engage in gainful occupations, with priority for veterans and special services for handicapped persons.

The State Employment Services, affiliated with the US Employment Service, provide for the designation of at least one staff member in each of the nearly 2,500 local Job Service Offices throughout the country; he is responsible for ensuring that handicapped jobseekers receive all available special services. The principal services include: appraisal of handicapped jobseekers' interests, abilities, etc.; evaluation of handicapped persons' physical and mental capacities; referral to institutional, on-the-job, or remedial education training; referral to other agencies for supportive services; analysis of jobs; providing a wide range of high-priority services to veterans.

The existing rehabilitation and employment service provisions all operate to enhance employment opportunities for handicapped persons;

- the Community Service Employment Pilot Programme provides full- or part-time community employment to handicapped persons referred by state vocational rehabilitation agencies. The Labor Department is authorised to enter into agreements with public and private non-profit agencies, including national organisations and state and local governments to conduct pilot projects;

- projects with industry is a programme whereby the Federal Government may enter into agreements with individual employers to establish jointly-financed projects that deliver training and employment services to physically and mentally handicapped persons;

- the job tax credit programme is an incentive measure for employers to employ disabled persons.

Finally, the President's Committee on Employment of the Handicapped was established in 1947 to help the handicapped help themselves. This is accomplished through various national education and information programmes.

As far as vocational rehabilitation personnel is concerned, grants are allocated to state agencies and other public or non-profit organisations, including institutions of higher education, to support training projects, traineeships and related activities designed to increase the number of qualified rehabilitation personnel. Vocational, medical, social and psychological components of rehabilitation services and also employment assistance are covered by the grants.

4. Research

A National Institute of Handicapped Research has been created as a separate administrative entity of the Rehabilitation Services Administration, but within the Department of Education. A network of research and training centres, developed in conjunction with institutions of higher education, is authorised to train rehabilitation professionals and researchers and to co-ordinate and conduct advanced research.

A Federal Interagency Committee has been established to identify and co-ordinate all federal rehabilitation research activities.

At present, the National Institute of Handicapped Research is preparing a comprehensive programme of specific studies which are to be carried out in the next few years.

URUGUAY

1. Legislative provisions

    -   Act No. 14640 (1957) [as amended by Act No. 14489/1975]
        provides for a Pilot Centre for Vocational Rehabilitation;

    -   Act No. 10401 provides for a percentage of vacant government
        posts to be filled by disabled;

    -   Decree No. 587 sets up the National Social and Labour
        Rehabilitation Council;

    -   Act No. 13892 (1970) provides in section 250 for special
        remuneration for instructors of handicapped persons;

    -   Decree No. 117 (1971) sets up the National Mental
        Rehabilitation Centre;

    -   Constitutional Decree No. 9 (1979) reorganises the social
        security scheme and sets up the Directorate of Social Security
        attached to the Ministry of Labour and Social Security. The
        system is now unified and previous measures (such as the Act
        establishing the State Insurance Bank) are repealed.

Other legislative provisions deal with various aspects of mental
retardation and psychopathology.

2. Vocational rehabilitation services

Apprenticeship and training in various trades are provided by the
Pilot Centre for Vocational Rehabilitation (CEPRO) under the Minstry
of Labour and Social Security.

Special care of different groups of handicapped (blind, deaf, mute)
is provided by numerous foundations and private associations. Among
them, the National Organisation for Disabled Workers promotes
vocational education for persons suffering from disorders of the
locomotive system.

3. Employment

Selective placement services are offered by the Pilot Centre for
Vocational Rehabilitation.

4. Special measures

    -   Free transport for disabled persons on buses (municipal
        regulations);

    -   exemption from import duties on motor vehicles and necessary
        spare parts;

    -   priority to blind married couples for housing loans from the
        Mortgage Bank.

5.   Research

Data on disabled persons exist only at the institutional level.   A
survey   at   the national level is planned and its results will serve
as a basis for a permanent system of collecting and processing   data
on disabled persons.

II.   ANALYSIS

The information contained in the foregoing summaries of 68
government replies to the ILO survey on rehabilitation legislation
and services gives only a general overview rather than a detailed
picture of recent developments. Moreover, with the rapid pace of
legislative action and expansion in services, any law-and-practice
report soon tends to become outdated. Frequently, and in many
countries, services for the disabled are running ahead of official
statutory provisions for their functioning. The International Year
of Disabled Persons (1981) accelerated this development.

The country replies, in general, confirm that over the past
decade the scope of rehabilitation services for the disabled has
been expanded in many parts of the world. A great many countries
have launched new specialised training, placement and employment
programmes, or built up existing ones.   Legislative and
administrative actions have created new government departments,
councils and similar bodies to serve the disabled. Non-governmental
and voluntary organisations have similarly widened their scope of
work, often with the help of government stimulus and support.
Increased resources have thus been earmarked for rehabilitation,
more rehabilitation workers have been recruited and trained, and the
public's awareness of the needs and potentials of disabled people
has been intensified.

The newer and developing countries have passed beyond the
initial stage of providing pilot services for the disabled in their
societies and have been active in developing rehabilitation centres
and workshops, some of them in rural areas. A few of them have
pioneered imaginative new schemes of job creation for their
disabled.

Industrialised countries, on the other hand, have been seeking
to advance the integration of the disabled into working and
community life, reaching out to the severely and multiply
handicapped, the mentally ill and socially maladjusted. Many
specialised provisions for vocational training and job placement
have been introduced; new regulations deal with the financing of the
complex and costly services, often within the framework of social
insurance systems. Special standards apply to the fast-developing
professionalisation of rehabilitation personnel, as well as to the
co-ordination of services in which the disabled themselves are
obtaining direct involvement. The growing application of advanced
technology to general and vocational training of the disabled, to
adaptation of work processes, to mobility, to communication, and to
general daily living have posed special questions; among these are
how to plan the further development of these important aids, and how
to share costs of production and distribution for these often costly
sophisticated devices between users and the wider society.

The following additional comments refer to some specific
trends that emerged from the country replies.

1.   Rights of the disabled and the law

Several countries report guarantees that are contained in the
national Constitution, basic law, or similar documents. They cover
the right or duty to work, the right to health care, the right to

assistance in case of severe illness or impairment, the right to rehabilitation, or related rights. Understandably, some of these constitutional assurances lack specificity and still require the State to assure full implementation of the principles through appropriate statutes.

The defence of minority rights which has been a very important development in many countries can be found embodied in laws, some of which guarantee to disabled persons the right to equal opportunities in education, in employment, the right to physical access, and to protection against discriminatory measures. Other innovative provisions impose upon employers and organisations the obligation to establish "positive policies" or "affirmative action programmes", etc. to promote actively the integration of disabled persons. Some rehabilitation legislation, e.g. sections of the 1973 Rehabilitation Act in the United States, contain detailed monitoring systems to determine compliance with the integration policy and to set up grievance and complaint procedures for disabled persons charging discrimination.

2.   Scope_of_provisions_and
      eligibility_requirements

During the 1970s, many countries, notably the industrialised countries, have extended the scope of provisions to cover larger numbers of disabled persons for rehabilitation services. This includes statutory amendments or supplementary legislation, as well as administrative measures, to add other disability categories (e.g. mentally handicapped, mentally ill, alcohol- and drug-dependent persons, socially maladjusted), to decentralise services in order to reach rural disabled, to provide rehabilitation services to disabled women and elderly disabled; some industrialised countries also expanded eligibility requirements to include migrant foreign workers who had become disabled.

The world-wide emphasis on human rights that marked the last decade includes a growing international movement to serve the human rights of all individuals with disabling conditions. The 1976 United Nations Declaration on the Rights of Disabled Persons sounded a global call for national and international action in favour of the disabled. Since that time, the rehabilitation programmes of many countries have been expanded not only by governments but also with the active involvement of non-governmental organisations, employers, trade unions and voluntary associations. It is hoped that this impetus will be maintained as the long-term plan of action associated with the International Year of Disabled Persons gets under way.

3.   Vocational_rehabilitation
      and_social_security

The links between vocational rehabilitation services and social insurance systems (health insurance, accident insurance, unemployment insurance, disability insurance), which in the industrialised countries were established in the early decades of this century, have become strengthened. The connections and co-ordination apply to registration and referral of handicapped persons, the organisation of data on assessment, work experience and earnings and it involves the financing of benefits and services, the establishment of rehabilitation centres, sheltered workshops, specialised residential facilities, and over-all administrative supervision. In Eastern European socialist countries, as well as in many others, the legislation providing for rehabilitation of disabled persons is part of the existing social security system. The difficulties of employing disabled persons are especially serious in developing countries and thus the provision of assistance and services is still often the responsibility of social service departments or non-governmental organisations. Nevertheless, there is a trend to regard help to handicapped adults, whether it involves financial support or retraining and special work schemes, not as a question for social welfare but as a labour and employment issue. Since most social security systems are set up as work-related contributory schemes, the costs and controls of vocational rehabilitation efforts quite naturally relate to them. Recent legal and administrative provisions reflect this tendency. The question of coverage and availability of vocational rehabilitation and retraining services to the entire population has arisen in a number of countries. The Federal Republic of Germany for example has enacted far-reaching legislation in this respect, but even small nations (e.g. Fiji) have approached the issue through special financial and other legislative provisions.

Subsidy payments to employers that recruit, train and employ disabled persons are in some cases authorised under broad social security type provisions but more often are made possible through specialised arrangements of labour and employment services (e.g. in Finland).

In general, the country responses indicate a gradual move towards comprehensive rehabilitation legislation (e.g. Argentina, Egypt), but such co-ordination is still exceptional in the countries of the developing world. During the last decade, some ten countries have established national councils for the handicapped, usually by statute, to promote effective collaboration between government bodies and private organisations serving the disabled.

In the industrialised countries, the setting up of inter-departmental committees not only permits the co-ordination of activities at different government levels, and a control of the quality of services provided, but it signifies that the central government can play an important role in the development of new employment outlets (e.g. semi-sheltered enclaves in industrial undertakings) and in services to specific groups of disabled and disadvantaged (e.g. ex-prisoners). Several replies refer to inter-departmental committees and interministerial councils to promote the integration of the disabled in governmental employment.

4.   Training_and_employment

Replies indicate that many countries have strengthened state control of specialised guidance, training and employment services for disabled persons. The Employment and Training Act (1973) in the United Kingdom made the new Manpower Services Commission responsible for such training and placement programmes. Similar measures exist in the United States under the Comprehensive Employment and Training Act which subsidises training positions and jobs in a variety of occupations. State and local governments, and also private organisations which promote job preparation and employment opportunities for the disabled, can receive federal government funds but must have established approved affirmative action plans as required under federal law.

Several country replies refer to legislation on the establishment of special training centres and workshops, both for young persons with congenital impairments and for adult disabled (e.g. Denmark, USSR, United Kingdom). Particularly extensive networks of such rehabilitation facilities have been created under federal-state arrangements in the Federal Republic of Germany.

The job placement and employment of disabled persons have been adversely affected by the recent economic recession and high rates of unemployment. The difficulty of employing disabled persons is felt especially in developing countries. Legislative provisions therefore reflect the keen concern of the authorities with these severe difficulties, taking at times the form of preserving designated types of occupations, introducing or strengthening quota obligations or, where quota schemes are not effective or operative, offering financial and fiscal incentives to employers to retain disabled persons on their former or a more suitable job.

A number of European countries, notably those in Scandinavia, have pioneered programmes in which government departments, employers, trade unions and voluntary organisations co-operate to safeguard the jobs of those who become, or are at risk of becoming, disabled (e.g. Adjustment Group system in Sweden); in other cases, the schemes take the form of contracts between undertakings and the employment service (as in Norway) which provide, through rehabilitation committees, for the adaptation of jobs and the working environment so that disabled workers can become integrated into the regular workforce.

The adaptation of the working environment is itself a subject for legislation in a number of countries (e.g. Federal Republic of Germany, Sweden, USSR, United Kingdom). These provisions deal with the supply of assistive devices and other adjustments, as well as the technical and financial provisions to make them available to disabled users. New regulations apply to the protection of residual capacities, for example the appropriate adaptation of workplaces for workers with sensorial limitations (e.g. USSR). This new legislation is linked to other statutes of disability prevention, reduction of work accidents, work safety and health for all workers.

Some countries have regualted the placement of handicapped jobseekers into general employment (so-called "mainstreaming" in the United States). Government departments, under new legislation in some countries, provide subsidies and incentives to employers that co-operate in the programme. There are also examples where such state assistance has been combined with specific collective bargaining agreements between undertakings and trade unions (e.g. Federal Republic of Germany). Quota laws often have penalty clauses under which employers who do not achieve the stipulated percentage must make certain payments. In some countries, the contributions that are thus collected are placed into a fund from which additional rehabilitation services can be financed. New legislative developments have made state control of placement procedures more effective through increase in the mandatory payments and through new devices such as trial work periods, probationary periods to provide greater flexibility for potential employers and to reduce work disincentives for disability pensioners.

Countries which have adopted quota schemes have varying percentage requirements, but usually ranging from 2 per cent to 4 per cent for undertakings with 20 to 100 employees. The disability categories that are protected may be defined broadly (e.g. Turkey) or may be restricted to persons with a certain degree of disability (e.g. Austria). Sometimes only the public sector is affected (e.g. Greece), but usually private undertakings are the main target of the provisions. Several countries have decided to modify or set aside the use of quota schemes because of their relative inefficiency (e.g. New Zealand).

A considerable number of replies refer to special workshops and sheltered facilities. The legislation deals with the central allocation of work contracts, with the application of standards for operation, and with the payment of wages. Where employers or organisations operating sheltered and special workshops pay workers less than the statutory minimum wage, this must be authorised under exception clauses. The organisation of special workshops has been further elaborated in some countries under additional provisions that enable regular undertakings to create sheltered or semi-sheltered "enclaves" within their normal production activities. These have been set up under special support and subsidy provisions of the legislation concerning training, placement and employment of handicapped workers.

Another important trend, evident from government replies, is the development of home-work schemes in industrialised countries (e.g. Poland and USSR) as well as in developing countries (e.g. Malaysia).

Co-operatives of disabled which are frequently established in Eastern European countries, but also for example in Burma and India, represent an important and interesting structure which provides a wide range of services suited to the needs of disabled persons. The movement has been expanding. For example, Ecuador, Portugal and Spain have included the preparation of relevant provisions in their future plans.

5.   Community participation and support

The current situation of disabled persons in nearly all countries calls not only for the development of job opportunities but also for enlarged public understanding and positive attitudes in the community. This applies to all categories of disabled but especially to those with severe impairments, the multiply handicapped, and other groups that suffer from special discrimination (e.g. leprosy sufferers, epileptics, the mentally ill and mentally retarded). Thus, the success of integration is not only dependent upon legislative, administrative provisions for material and financial assistance to the disabled. Public education and information, the involvement of community groups in the implementation of training and employment schemes, notably representatives of the disabled themselves, take on great significance. In this context, trade unions have a key position and can play a major role in the development of national employment policies. Some countries have developed special systems of co-operation between government and trade unions. An illustration is Hungary where the Ministry of Labour and the National Council of Trade Unions have issued joint guidelines on rehabilitation services provided by enterprises and administrative authorities. Community participation in social rehabilitation and integration, such as for example in Canada, is an important step forward in providing much-needed support for the reintegration and rehabilitation of disabled persons into active social and economic life. Employers and their organisations likewise made important efforts and contributions to vocational rehabilitation activities both at governmental and private levels. The support given by private enterprises in the United States to the National Industries for the Blind (which itself is a very large workshop system under public provisions) is an outstanding example of co-operation and community support for vocational rehabilitation activities.

In conclusion, and with a view towards the future plans and research activities reported in the replies, many governments seek to explore new ways of providing suitable job training and employment opportunities. It is evident, however, that new sources for the financing of training programmes which match up to new job requirements be found, and the achievements of modern technology must be made accessible to all disabled who require technical aids and assistive devices, but above all there must be a continuing sensitising of public opinion to ensure support for efforts aimed at abolishing discrimination and affirming the rights of the disabled to an equal share of employment opportunities.